Going Round The Bend On The QE2
by
Nicholas Walker

ISBN: 9781520175973

Books By Nicholas Walker
Mass Market
The Ice Mountain
Skating on Thin Ice
Black Belt
Tie Break
Jazz Dancer
The Boy Who Was Afraid of Heights
Crackling Ice
Skating on the Edge
The Touch of the Ice
Together on Ice
Surprise Surprise (anthology)
Getting to Grips With Grammar
Getting to Grips With Grammar Two
Kindle
<u>Books for Younger Children</u>
Daniel Gerzergerblad and the Incidences
Barnaby Cole, Detective
Arnold, the World's Greatest Swordtoad
Tick, Tock and Toby
Replay
Gordon the Nervous Ghost and Other Stories

<u>Books for Older Children/Young Adults</u>
Dancing With the Enemy
Children of the Kraal
Heaven's Avenger
Heaven's Avenger Two…the Gates of Jericho
Kisses in the Dark

Dance Academy
Spiral Staircase
Help me Make it Through the Night

<u>Books for Adults</u>
Going Around the World on the QE2 (autobiographical)
Not Quite Sane in America (autobiographical)
Losing My Marbles in L A (2016)
Kiss Mommy Goodbye
A Better Way to Die
Painted Smile
Sillouettes in the Dark
Dancing in the Dark
The Poisoner's of Moloo and other Science Fiction Stories

<u>Technical and Scientific</u>
Kicking the Crap out of the Martial Arts
Dieting is for Idiots
How to Pass any Exam With One Night's Revision
120 of the Best Lessons Plans From Kernow Karate

Prologue

'Sweetheart,' I said tenderly, 'I know I've been working too hard and I've got a bit stressed, but that is all in the past now. If we both try hard and remember how much we loved each other we can make our marriage work again.' I gave her my very best smile, the one she said always made her go weak, and those perfect lips in that angelic face opened:

'I want you to sod off just as soon as you can…sooner!'

It was the trunk that gave me the idea. I was walking around Ingatestone the following morning wondering where in the world I should go. I considered going to my Mother's but then again she doesn't approve of me much more than The Poison Dwarf does. I felt spoilt for choice, I could sit down on the bench by the bread shop and have a brief cry or perhaps lay down in the graveyard until someone came and asked me the impossible question: ***Just what the hell do you think you are doing?*** Still, the Quack said that this feeling would fade but was evasive when I tried to pin him down to a time frame.

    And then I saw the trunk. It was in the window of the antique shop, the one that never had anything interesting to buy. It's a place I like to visit from time to time, I don't buy anything I just like to open wooden boxes and crush the dried flowers, that sort of thing. But today I had a mission, I marched in proudly, today I was going to buy! I wandered around the trunk, opened the bulging lid, it was wooden and satisfyingly large like you could hide a body inside. I haggled with the sweet old lady and, after fifteen minutes got it for exactly the price she first asked for, and heaved it outside and up onto my roof rack. I sat in the car and toyed with ideas for a moment, should I kill The Poison Dwarf and hide her body in the trunk? Should I try going over Niagara Falls in it? Both ideas had their merits but instead I phoned up my friend Christine.

    Now Christine is just an ordinary girl to me, a member of my club, a friend…but to everybody else she is the managing director of one of the largest travel agents in the country. An ordinary mortal cannot get to speak to her but I have her special number.

'How are you Beautiful? Are you busy?' I said.

'Busier than you,' she said. 'Things going any better?'

'They are truly tremendous, every day I leap from my bed screaming with joy at the thought of yet another day,' said I. 'Listen kid, I once read an article on the QE2 and I was wondering about how you go about getting on the World cruise…I mean when does it start? And from where?'

'Are you serious?'

'Oh, I'm rarely serious, you know that,' I said, 'but it's either that or Niagara Falls.'

'Niagara Falls?'
'No, the QE2.'
'Can you afford it?'
'Probably not, but then who cares?'

She sighed, 'I'll be honest with you Nick, I can probably get you on it but the World cruise lasts for over four months.'

'Great! Let's do it. When does it start?'

'Well, my dear Nick, The QE2 sails from Southampton tomorrow morning on the start of it's World cruise.'

So I packed me trunk and said goodbye to the circus. Not wishing to seem rude I left a post it note on the fridge for her:

Elizabeth, Your dinner is in the oven...
*** I am going away for a time. Nick***

And I ran away around the world, on the QE2.

1) Southampton

Southampton's not a place you go is it? I mean, you don't go there for a holiday, or you don't hear people saying: ***Grandma's coming down for the weekend, we simply must take her to Southampton!*** But it's big, you know, so somebody must go there. The ships are even bigger and biggest of them all is The Queen Elizabeth II.

I've got the best daughter in the world, she always has been, but even more since The Poison Dwarf started playing up. That's not to say she's the best driver. To be brutally frank she's bloody awful! The car came to a shuddering halt with a screech of brakes and a tirade of questionable language from a passing cyclist. After a decent pause I pulled my hands away from my eyes and started breathing again.

'You know,' I said, conversationally, 'I think he got seven adjectives into that sentence.'

She gave me that sweet smile that meant she had just dropped the telly out of the window or flogged the flymo (again!). 'I expect he was just having a bad day,' she said. She gestured with her head, 'I think that's it.' And that's when I realised it was so big, I mean you don't really think of ships being that big, do you? There was a boy down our road when I was a kid who had a model of it (well, he had a model of everything he did, little shit) and it didn't look anything like.

'Dad, you are sure you want to do this?' she asked in her little girl's voice.

'Oh, I've got to now,' I said, climbing out of the car, 'Mum said I'd never go through with it and I'd certainly rather die than prove her right.'

'But the doctor says you're in the middle of a nervous breakdown,' she said, 'who's going to look after you on the QE2?'

'I'm going to look after me,' I said portentously, probably the only thing I've ever said portentously in my whole life. 'That's the whole point, it's not up to you to look after your father!'

'Well, who else is going to do it?' she demanded. 'Elizabeth won't!'

'Exactly!' said I. 'Now, listen Sweetheart, if you want to look after me, you look after getting some help with all this luggage.'

Jaime sighed, and in that infuriating capable way she has, whistled up a brace of porters who started unloading the bits of my luggage that were still attached to the car after her driving adventures. We both had a brief hug and a brief cry and I wandered off up the gangplank. Plank? Damn, I was exhausted by the time I reached the top. A nice lady with lots of teeth and breasts welcomed me with much rehearsed fulsomeness and showed me to my cabin, number 444. I stood looking around it still a bit dazed, how my life had changed in just a few short days! Two weeks ago I had been a married man with a beautiful young wife and a beautiful baby daughter with a big house and a position as lecturer at the university. What was I doing here? I shrugged and popped one of the pills the Quack had said should keep me from going completely off my trolley and checked my cabin out. It was okay. Christine had got me seriously upgraded and I had a double cabin with a tiny office space and a porthole. The porthole was to become a snare and a delusion as you never could see anything out of it because of the spray and you obviously couldn't open it…but I liked having it because I knew it cost a few extra thousand just to get a cabin with a porthole. I'd be able to swank at all the parties: **Yes, you might well be knight but have you got a porthole?... Hey there baby, would you like to come back to my cabin and look out of my porthole?**

Best of all, on the tiny desk, was a bottle of chilled champagne with a note from Christine and her sister Jacqui wishing me love and luck. I was so taken aback by this that I had another short cry followed by a long drink to wash down some more of the magic pills.

Trouble is I don't really drink and after half a bottle I went for a stagger around the ship. Yes it is really big! Yet, everything is very near, if you want to nip back to your cabin for something (if, that is, you can find your cabin) it's only a minute away. The gym, the swimming pool, the hospital are all just an elevator ride away.

The ship was full of hoards of older people, I was later to learn that at forty seven I was the youngest on the World cruise, and I went around looking for women. No, nothing really like that, I just wanted someone to be nice to me. After the abrupt break up of my marriage I needed some reassurance. But I didn't find much, there were many more women than men but they all appeared to be in their seventies, it was a bit of a culture shock because the Poison Dwarf had been twenty years younger than me. I went through the Red Lion pub and across to the side windows to see the people still boarding and this film star carrying a massive painting bumped into me.

'Oh sorry,' said a British voice. 'This is heavier than it looks.'

'Kandinsky always did use too much paint,' said I.

'Good grief,' said those amazing lips, 'an art connoisseur?'

'I can't even spell connoisseur,' I said, 'I just have an interest in modern art, it's such a marvellous way of annoying people.'

She gave a truly great smile, 'Yeah, it is a bit,' she said. 'I'm the art auctioneer on board, we hold auctions three days a week...you should try it.'

'Only if you take your knickers off for me,' I said, but not aloud. Instead I came out with an inspired piece of repartee: 'I'll make sure of it,' I said and walked away. No, no, no, she was much too perfect, I'm short, fat and ugly and I'm not going to get anywhere with a goddess. But damn she was perfect, what I wouldn't give to take her back to the Poison Dwarf and say: 'Look what I've found.' Now that would be immature, but on the other hand I like being immature...the people who really piss me off are the ones who take life so seriously all the damn time.

But it was getting dangerous, members of the QE2 staff (you can spot them by their red jackets and their extra teeth) were on the prowl looking out for any unattached passengers with nothing to do...they throw a net over them and drag them off to the icebreaker party and show them magic tricks until they give them the secret plans! Fortunately, I have a friend on the escape committee and I slunk off back to my cabin for a sleep and a sulk.

2) The Atlantic

     I've effortlessly made myself the most unpopular person on board within the first hour, that's got to be some sort of record even for me! To avoid the introduction stuff, all that ghastly meeting of people, I hid in my cabin and lay on my bed with my earplugs in. They worked okay but the insistent, even incessant spiel from the overhead speaker still kept me awake even though I couldn't actually hear what was being said. I was getting annoyed as the ship was now over an hour late starting when there came a furious knocking on the door. An agitated little man informed me that everyone had been at lifeboat stations for the mandatory practise drill for over an hour now and the whole ship was waiting for me…oh dear. When I slunk in the back of my meeting room I never felt so many eyes deliberately avoiding mine!

We started off across the Atlantic in the worst weather anyone, including the Captain, could remember. Big C was talking about hurricane force gales at one point. Everyone was sick including most of the crew. I wasn't too bad but I decided to have the magic injection everyone was talking about as the navigator was threatening it was going to get worse. Well, that wasn't the real reason, there's no point to this journal unless I keep to the truth. I did have an ulterior motive, then again I usually do have an ulterior motive, rumour had it that the nurse was worth a second look, well worth seventy-five pounds anyway! I was greeted by a smashing bit of stuff whose first words were to drop my trousers, I replied that I was game if she was and she yawned and told me to bend over the bed. I told her that I wasn't really into that being more of a sadist than a masochist but I would try anything once, bar, of course, morris dancing. She told me to shut up or she would check out my prostrate while I was in situ as it were and proceeded to plunge an inordinately long needle deep into my fixed assets. I tell you, the whole medical profession has a bum fixation, half the reason for me running away was because my doctor was insisting I had an operation on mine (yes, the painful one). She told me that she had seen over a hundred bare bottoms that day and I decided to strike her off my Christmas card list…you'd be in an intimate moment with that one and suddenly you'd remember where her hands had been all day…and what if she found some worrying lump when you were in the throes? No, no, no I like my women more grateful than that.

Dinner is the big event of the day. You can eat all day long if you want, and certainly some people seem to do this: there's all the normal meals from breakfast right up to an evening supper which you have to go to whether you are hungry or not just to admire the gateaux that the chefs compete amongst themselves to create: there was one made entirely out of tiny skulls (false ones, well, I hope they were false ones) a bit too macabre for my taste but there was also one of an entire brass band so I ate three trumpeters. And then there's the ice sculptures, some of these are truly incredible and are the size of a small car. There's always a restaurant open and anyway, it's immaterial because you can ask for your meals to be served in your cabin at any time of day or night. But, like I say, dinner is the big occasion. You dress up in evening wear and go down to experience the world's best service.

My first dinner was less than totally successful. Surprisingly, considering the weather, the Mauritania restaurant was packed. Typical, people are as sick as parrots but they still manage to stagger down for their fodder…though I've never really understood the origins of the parrot phrase, are parrots particularly noted for their weak stomachs? Anyway, I was a bit late, what with having my bum prodded and all so I was sat at a big round table with a mixed group of people who all evidently recognised me from the boat drill fiasco. I was just glaring suspiciously at my companions to see whom I was likely to fall out with when the ship stood on one end. The people either side of me went arse over tit but with my lightening reflexes and speed of thought I calmly reached for the two glasses of water in front of me as I went over backwards and lay there smugly not spilling a drop. The flower vase got me first with a huge smash of cold water followed shortly by the brown sugar so I was left looking like I had some horrible brown growth all over me. The two old ladies who had fallen either side of me were obviously ex-circus performers because they each rolled nimbly to their feet and calmly took their places back at the table which the ever vigilant bus boys were already putting to rights. The one I admired most though was the loud Texan who lifted his plate just as the table went over, waited with Chesterfieldian calm for it to be put back again, then casually went on eating without even a break in his conversation. I slunk away from the happy gathering to have a much needed wash and brush up. I distinctly heard one elderly lady, as I crept past her table, demanding to know what it was I was suffering from and was it catching…I never did find out where my sirloin went.

    Things, however, picked up the next day. I was attempting to slide my photograph out of the ship's display (it makes me look even a bigger idiot than I really am) when this pompous German shouldered me aside. I decided, hell, I was on holiday so ignore it, and he promptly did it again, I mean really did it like an American footballer going for the quarterback. I put my hand on his shoulder and took him to where we could see the sea rushing past and asked him politely whether he could swim. He: ***Sprechen zie nicht English*** so I taught him how to say: ***Excuse me please!*** He learned it too because for the rest of the week he used it every time he saw me. I must have been a bit fraught at the time because it appears quite a few people overheard this segment of social intercourse and my popularity with everybody seems to have gone through the roof. It appears that the German gentleman (is that an oxymoron?) seems to have rubbed rather a lot of people up the wrong way. The barman even slipped me a long thin cigar, I wonder what I would have got if I had chucked him over the side…ten years I expect.

    I feel I have descended into a deeper and more dreadful world! Things were going so well, I'd spent the five days crossing to New York persuading myself that it wasn't a dream it was really me doing this mad thing…I was really here. I'd settled into a nice little routine: training, eating, swimming, writing, watching the evening movie, when disaster struck: there's this woman after me!

    It happened like this. I was press ganged into going to the single's party, I mean it was impossible to refuse. I tried telling everyone that I was a sexual neuter, a homophobe, a heterophobe, a woman hater, a man hater, but everyone just keeps insisting, if your not getting laid regular then you have to go to the single's party…it's the law! So I went late and sat in the corner having a sulk while these annoying little fourteen year-old crew members tried to get us to play party games. One cheerfully idiotic girl wanted me to go around with a piece of paper trying to find somebody else who had the same birthday as me, my reply was so rude that her smile, even though it had been stitched on by QE2 seamstresses, slipped an inch. Well, I was sidling out when this huge woman pounced, I struggled madly but she brought me down like an All Black defender handling an attack on his base line.

    She's about forty and not unattractive in a statuesque kind of way, but she whistles through her teeth and calls me Nikky-Mate…obviously she is an Australian. And her teeth have to be seen to be believed! I know I always go on about people's teeth but she's got twice the normal allotted amount, they overlap at the front and there's extra ones in front of those and when she laughs (all the time) she looks like a Siberian tiger ripping a steak off the rump of a passing caribou. But that's not the worst, she giggles whenever you are talking and when she makes a point she winks roguishly…oooh, it's ghastly! You sit there waiting, thinking, 'And now the wink.' And bang! She never fails to deliver.

    I am at a decided disadvantage because I don't know her name and for once it's not my fault. When she meets you for the first time she grabs your hand in a gorillalike grip, hauls on it like she is testing a mooring rope and as you are catapulted forward she bawls in your face something like sounds likes: **Stoke!** Now I dunno, but are even Australians named Stoke? You can hardly blame me for not knowing her name, it's exactly like having your hand caught in the sliding door of a train just as it's pulling out into a force ten gale and expecting you to grasp what the station announcer is saying at the same time.

    I've taken to darting in and out of state rooms and eating at odd times to avoid her. Consequentially, there's a kind of sub class of passengers I have entered into, the elderly loonies, they eat strange foods in strange places at strange times, the ordinary passenger never comes into contact with them. The most worrisome part of the whole thing is the way in which they so readily welcome me into their ranks waving their bread crusts and showing their gums. One kindly old gentleman took his teeth out yesterday to show me. I can't work out which is worst, the loonies or the roguish winker…at least the loonies don't have any designs on my body.

    She waited by the gangplank at New York but fortunately I have developed a kind of sixth sense and spotted her through my porthole…ha ha! My steward Lito smuggled me out through a loading bay and I entered New York on the front of a fork lift truck. Lito will do anything for me partly because it's his job and partly because I've got the goods on him. Still, I've only got to make it to Fort Lauderdale and she's gone. Lito? Well, we had Christmas at sea and everybody went out on the boat deck to see Christmas in and dance until…well, you get the idea. I danced until the small hours last Christmas and had the worst year of my life so this year I slunk off to my cabin and read a book. Then when everybody had staggered drunkenly off to bed I went for one of my solitary prowls, something I've been doing since I was a kid. At about 3 o clock I watched three drunken Filipinos smuggling the antique ship's bell into the laundry room and one of them was Lito. The following morning, amongst all the hue and cry I dropped in to see him in his cubby hole, he was sitting on a tea chest clutching his head and groaning. When I mentioned the bell to him he shot bolt upright like the nurse had been at him and you could see from the frantic look in his eyes he was thinking: *So it wasn't a dream!* How on earth he is intending to get it back is beyond me, it must weigh a ton. Now when I want anything I just murmur: *Ding Dong.*

3) New York

I got up early as per orders from Big C to view the New York skyline. It was big and impressive and well worth getting up for, so having seen it I went back to bed. The big disappointment was the Statue of Liberty, it's not nearly as big as you think it's going to be…and it's stuck out there on this insignificant island, not at all where you think it is: it's a bit like putting Big Ben on Sark! My theory is that when Eiffel and Bartholdi designed it the

French were so appalled at the thought of having another monstrosity like the Eiffel Tower on their hands that they shipped it off to America and called it a gift, ask yourself why else would the French give anything away? The poor trusting Americans riveted it all together (it's made up of copper panels, a bit like a posh Airfix kit really) and even they realized how dreadful it was so they stuck it way off on Liberty island to try and cut down on the number of immigrants. It all backfired of course because she has enormous breasts and the entire American nation has a fixation about breasts.

It's a bit odd, we visit New York for one day then cruise around the Caribbean for a few days then return to New York to pick up more passengers so you have to cram everything into two lots of about eight hours. I didn't expect to like New York but I did. It's not a bit like London, there's large spaces between the shops and it's dead easy to find your way around because it's built in a grid fashion. There seems to be an inordinately large number of huge black women with enormous breasts (I told you). It's unwise to walk too closely behind one of them because they are likely to swing around and smash you into the street where you no doubt get squashed by one of America's incredibly long lorries (what is it Americans have that they need such impractical transport? Answers on a postcard). The people are lovely and so polite, they say it's because they expect to get shot if they're rude to anyone. Best of all…best of all!!! On every street corner there is a pretzel seller, they're wonderful, they cost $1 and you can still be eating them twenty minutes later. It had been snowing in New York for days and there were big piles of snow everywhere. I walked into this black man while staring up at the skyscrapers, this is very common and immediately reveals you as a tourist, and he collapsed back into a snowdrift. I was very apologetic, after all if possible I did not wish to get shot, but it sort of turned into a pantomime because he was so fat he couldn't get back up and kept slipping over again. A crowd gathered around him all trying to be sympathetic while I staggered around hooting with laughter: 'Open your eyes man, open your eyes!' I don't know what happened whether they sent for lifting apparatus or waited for the thaw because I crept away and had another pretzel.

    I went for a stroll up the Empire State Building but the queues for the tickets were unbelievable, I bet Cary Grant didn't have to pay! I stormed out in a rage and a huge voice roared out: 'Nikky-mate.' Oh shit, she's found me! The over-fanged Australian was on my track. Immediately I took off like Sebastian Coe across six lanes of traffic, just as everybody does in London. Dear me, there was a kerfuffle! Every driver in a radius of three miles slammed on their brakes and leaned on their horns. Do you know you can be fined for jaywalking? I mean actually be fined $80? This very annoyed cop gave me a very stern warning and I crept away from literally thousands of accusing eyes…I was only crossing the bloody road. I left a manuscript with a friendly agent then went into Saks to buy a dinner jacket and staggered out screaming when I was quoted over $1000! Fortunately I found the Men's Warehouse and a lady fitted me with one for under $200, she didn't seem to speak English, kept insisting on calling it a tuxedo, that's a junction isn't it? The jacket needed a slight alteration and they promised to do it in an hour if I would call back.

    So off to the MOMA (Museum of Modern Art), Paula (the modern art goddess) had told me where it was, good job too because the taxi driver sure as hell didn't know. Sadly it was all one big disappointment, not as good as the Tate and certainly nowhere near the Pompidou, it's all ultra modern with masses of photographs. It cost me $10 to get in and ten minutes to look around...the finest collection of modern art in the world my backside! Still it was nice to see Les Demoiselle and the like for real. I bought a poster of a Jackson Pollack painting, it was priced at $100 but I claimed to be a poor art student and showed my card for the Educational Institute and it came right down to $28. I walked down Fifth Avenue and saw the Rockefeller Centre where they do the ice skating and all the Christmas lights were still up so it was really very pretty. It was time to get my dinner jacket and, as I said, the second best thing about New York (other than the pretzels) is the way it is so easy to find your way around. Easy that is if you can remember the name of the shop! It took one taxi driver, one mounted cop and a paramedic half an hour before a little old lady suggested I look on the credit card receipt and amazingly I still had it. Then the cop I had met so warmly earlier in the day appeared, 'Say aren't you that crazy Englishman who can't cross the road?' I just managed to avoid getting shot when they discovered I was on the QE2 and everything was forgiven, 'You on the Queey man?' By this time it was a thick blizzard and everyone was standing around shaking my hand. The taxi driver finally rescued me and took me to get my jacket and the same thing happened there when they found out about the QE2. I felt almost like a celebrity as I swaggered through the fitting room people slapping me on the back and shaking my hand. I've said it before that Americans are the nicest people in the world.

The taxi driver, who looked like Sonny Listen, refused to go as far as the docks as it was too rough so he dropped me off by a breaker's yard and I started to walk. I was congratulating myself on getting through the day without being shot or mugged when I realised a rather menacing looking black youth was following me very, very closely. Typically the area was bereft of other people, in fact he was to be congratulated on picking the ideal location to mug someone. I crossed the road, so did he, I speeded up, so did he…oh shit. I slowed down and he came real close so taking a deep breath I whirled around keeping low to duck under the attack, surprisingly his neck was wide open so I grabbed it, crashed him back against a chain link fence and drew back my other fist.

'What's your game pal?' I demanded (Clint Eastwood always calls them pal).

'Oh no, Dr Walker, don't hit me,' he howled. Yes it was Petey the steward off my deck, poor sod just out from the Philippines and the first time ashore and he has the bad judgment to follow me back to the ship. There came a growl from behind the fence and an enormous Rottweiler threw itself at the chain link. It was all too much and Petey broke down. Why do I feel so guilty? I herded him back to the ship then spotted a US aircraft carrier in the next dock so went to have a look and right there on the pointed end was the Blackbird. Yes **the Blackbird,** America's ultra secret, invisible fighter plane. I reached for my camera and an unnoticed American soldier reached for his armalite. 'No photographs, sir,' he said through his gum. I tried telling him I was harmless, then that there had been a program on the Discovery channel about The Blackbird but he stopped calling me sir, and obviously a keen Clint Eastwood fan, changed to Pal. I trolled off muttering the only Russian words I know: **Lublos lublu** (it means I love you…very handy if you happen to be in Minsk) but the undereducated sod just gobbed in the Hudson and disappeared back into his silo.

Big C had ordered us to view the exit from New York from the boat deck but it was freezing. I mean, really freezing! But I popped out in the dark for two minutes and stayed two hours. If I see nothing else on this journey then it's been worth it. Surely one of the most majestic sights in the world is to see those millions of lights amidst the snow. Even the Statue of Liberty looked better. Finally I staggered inside suffering from frostbite in all my extremities, and I do mean all! I bumped into Paula in the bar.

'You look a tad cold,' she said from behind a glass of champagne.

'I can't feel my teeth,' I gasped. 'I need a woman to warm my hands on.' She kindly, yet chastely, did her best. Yet it was an hour later standing in a hot shower before all my extremities came back to life and sadly then I was alone.

There are three really stunning women on board, I mean we are talking seriously beautiful here. The first one is the aforementioned Paula, the art auctioneer. Now I like modern art, and beautiful women, so I started going to the auctions from the first and surprisingly, because I was such an introverted, miserable, little turd, when I came aboard, (in contrast to now when I'm an extroverted, miserable big turd), she started bothering with me from day one. Then there's Daniella, the dance lady who moves like Darcy Bussel, she's Paula's best friend and is married to Warren, but neither of them are working at it. Then, there's Dorcus, (ugh! Might as well be called Mavis), who is the cocktail waitress in the Red Lion and in spite of her ungenerous name has a smile that makes you feel like one of those daft dogs that pee up your legs on the beach.

Well, these three form a kind of clique and I seem to have become included in it and as the eldest is only about 28 then I smell trouble and I know that the common sense thing to do is to steer clear, but as the great Jean Brodie said: ***I leave common sense to common people!***

4) Fort Lauderdale

She's gone, ha ha, she's gone! She came knocking at my cabin door last night. At least I think it was her, if it was Paula then I may have to kill myself. I huddled under the blankets shaking with fear. Then this morning I had breakfast in bed, because I knew she was getting off, until

Lito came and told me she'd been spotted lumbering down the gangplank.

Speaking of breakfast, the food on board is amazing. I wasn't going to eat at night, I thought I'd come back lean and fit but you can't not eat. If you're offered Chateaubriand followed by baked Alaska with Morello cherries you'd be mad not to try wouldn't you? They serve the Alaska with full ceremony, lights out and all the waiters bearing the flaming dishes aloft to the sound of the band, magnificent. Americans serve something called Prime Rib which they are convinced is what the English eat all the time, they gaze at me in bewilderment when I say I've never heard of it, incidentally, it appears that anything English is the height of chic. Anyway, Prime Rib is just a very thick, and I mean **thick,** slice of roast beef…and I can't resist it. I don't usually have a dessert but last night they were so good I passed on the main course and had three: Bailey's Irish Cream soufflé; fresh strawberries with Kirsch and choux pastry swans; and blueberry bread and butter pudding with brandy custard.

I eat at the late sitting, 8.30 – 9.30, about half the time it's formal, dinner jacket, long dresses, then we have informal which is jacket and tie, then in port it's casual. It's all great fun actually and the ladies look wonderful but the great thing is that most of your dinner companions change every week. At the last change I asked the restaurant manager whether he could fill my table with young women and I think he's taking the piss because I'm the youngest person on it.

I've got a very good table though, one of the large round ones that sits right in the centre of the Mauritania restaurant. The Mauritania is the place to be, the Queens serves exactly the same food but is stuffier. My table seats eight, and it is *my* table because I am on the World cruise and it is already referred to as Dr Walker's table. The people sitting on it are this week's problem! Opposite me sits a tiny black American woman named Arletta. She's about the best of the bunch, we have splendidly vigorous arguments while everybody else views us in horror. The other night we were in the middle of one when two new ladies were shown to the table. I was in full flow: 'My father wouldn't even sit at the same table as you! You belong to so many minority groups that's it's unreal: you're American, and black, and short, and a woman…'

'Being a woman's not a minority group,' she said waving a fork at me.

'To my father it is,' I said. 'And you're not grateful how readily I accept you as an equal. Three times I've asked you to do my laundry and three times you've refused!'

'I haven't got any rocks to smash it on,' said Arletta bleakly. The two ladies looked at each other nervously then in complete unison they stood up and went over to talk to the restaurant manager. When I next saw them they were dining at a table in the Queens Restaurant and they sort of ducked when they noticed me.

On my left is a tiny little American woman of 84 called May, she is just like one of the two old ladies out of Fawlty Towers, well both of them really. She gets passionately excited about things like where the butter's from and as most of the others are half deaf then you can imagine just how long these invigorating conversations take across the table. On my other side is B (I dunno) the lady who lives permanently on the ship, she was on a World cruise with her husband and he died so they buried him at sea and she just stayed on. B's alright but her delight is giving people information about the ship and this palls after a time. Malcolm, her son, sits next to her, her family take it in turns to visit her for a week on board, it's a good arrangement. As Malcolm told me, it costs under $50,000 a year, she's protected, fed, has the best medical service literally one deck below and can go dancing every night, and as he says, she's very short sighted and a retirement home in the States would cost twice as much. Trouble is he's a pathological adviser and I am aware that I am the biggest Know All onboard but I do try and keep my comments within areas where I do have some rudimentary knowledge. Sadly Malcolm does not view a complete lack of knowledge of any subject as a barrier from him being an instant expert.

Next to him sits Edna an English ex-headmistress. She's a bit upper class with the biting voice of her trade, I can see Edna caning me for my own good any day, but she has a wonderfully cynical sense of humour that helps me get through another one of Malcolm's monologues about the dignity of Congress. I liked her even more when she got slightly drunk at Big C's party and frightened the waiter…he's since changed tables.

Now we come to the real beauties of the group, Sid and James. They're both ex-Members of Parliament and if I ever had aspirations on standing for parliament then they have put the lid on them. Sid's gone now since he had a nasty go at the little Filipino waitress and made her cry. I shut him up and told him he was a bully, he asked to be moved to another table, and he was the best of the pair. James, oh shit James! Upper class, ex-army, rich, conceited, all this I can take, but he is without question the most boring person I have ever met in my life. He talked one evening for twenty two minutes straight on how he filled in his Christmas cards – truly! Twenty two sodding minutes, Edna and I timed him. He always starts with the words: ***Now this will interest you.*** I keep assuring him that he's wrong about this but he's too thick-skinned to care.

I'd asked to be moved but it's ***my*** table and they all like me, really they do. They keep turning up all over the ship and joining me. They sort of live vicariously through my latest exploits. Sometimes I think I'll be diving 30 metres down under the Caribbean and I'll hear those dreaded words: ***Nick, now this will interest you!***

The next port was Fort Lauderdale. I'm not mad keen on these organised trips, I mean if I were visiting a town in Britain I wouldn't automatically go round the local museum and china factory so why should I do that elsewhere? But I wanted to see the Cape Kennedy Space Center (that's how they spell it) so I handed over my $200 and trudged out to the bus. It was brilliant.

We were shown the biggest building in the world and just as we passed it the biggest doors in the World opened and there was the Space Shuttle precariously perched on its rear. We also saw the biggest vehicle in the World, the Crawler, the flat JCB that moves the shuttle around, even the tour host hadn't seen it before, it's only afterwards you realize that it was a piece of machinery that is about as interesting as a contraceptive machine. Then we went to the Space Garden, which contains all the rockets ever used in the space program…that can't be true can it? I mean what about the ones that blew up or are still in space? Next we went to the actual mission control centre for the Apollo program (the one you see in ***Apollo 13***) and were treated to a launch simulation. The thing that grabs you is that it's tiny, about the size of a garden shed. And all those computers, the guide was telling us that all those machines together could not do the things a modern day pocket calculator can do. We were allowed to walk through real pods for the space lab and everybody could view with fascinated horror the toilet arrangements. Lastly we were off to the biggest movie screen in the world. You sit up real close, sort of hanging there in the middle of the screen. They took us on a real filmed shuttle mission and you could almost reach out and touch the astronauts, which was sad because three of them were amongst the one's lost in the shuttle that crashed including Sally Ride, the teacher. It was without doubt the most exciting and memorable experience I have ever had at the movies (if you discount what happened with Sue from Woolworth's during ***The Good The Bad And The Ugly***).

    And then on the way home we were introduced to the most patronising commentator in the world! Oh shit, she was awful: 'Now this is the same road that all the workers at the centre come to work on in their cars.' 'Now you can see the ship so you can tell we're getting near.' 'Now if you look over to your right the three mile long runway that the Shuttle lands on is there…if only the trees were not in the way you could see it.' It wasn't just me everybody in the bus was shouting her down. When I got off I asked her if she had ever considered doing the commentary on ***the Teletubbies.*** 'Oh, do you think I would be any good at it?'

    'No, on second thoughts you're probably a bit young for them.'

    I was stunned to find that Fort Lauderdale was in Florida, well, suppose is in Florida because I presume it hasn't moved recently. Paula told me where it was, I didn't believe her because I thought that where they shot the rockets from was somewhere near New York but she showed me on a map. We were there two days so the next day I took a taxi to the Promenade, it's really quite impressive, there were masses of boats and moorings and bridges and other watery things…but mainly there are shops and shops and shops. Boy, was it busy? There were jazz bands and jugglers and magicians and escapologists, and so many people. You have to edge around the stalls sideways and if you go into an art gallery you're there for life: there is no way out! Why aren't these people at work? It was only later that I realized it was Sunday…duh!

  The whole area is just called **Downtown,** and it's obviously the place to be, or certainly the place to be if you happen to be a dog. Everybody is there showing their dogs off, it's like Crufts, only warm: there are those horrible big poodles with haircuts looking like homosexual peacocks, disdainful Afghan hounds cutting everybody dead…you just can't imagine them having a pee up a lamppost four sinister Dobermans eyeing you up like you're their next meal, two beautiful Bull Mastiffs taking their diminutive owner she new not where, (***Cromwell…Winston, now we don't want to go down here do we? Oh! Apparently we do***), and a gorgeous bulldog so fat his stomach dragged along the floor. You could go on and on, you could even get to like most of the dogs but the best bit was the batty owners: the one's that dressed like their dogs, all hairstyles and pink bows…ugh! The big tough men dragging ridiculous Pekingese along (***come on Princess Di, try and do a wee wee for daddy***), and the literally dozens of owners who walked along pulling baby carriages stuffed with smug dogs. Tell me have we got it wrong? If a alien from outer space came down to observe us and he saw one species washing and dressing the other, getting their food, transporting them and for Heaven's sake, picking up their excreta, which one would the alien think was in charge?

    I wandered around for over three hours then it was time to get a taxi back to the ship, bloody hell, I almost had to prostrate myself in front of one to get it to stop, I thought I was going to miss the ship! And the taxi driver: 'Say Bo, you jiving for the biiiig Queenie?' As I told him, 'I'm terribly sorry I only speak English.'

5) New York, New York

We've got a full day here this time, plenty of time to get into trouble, but actually I've decided to try and behave myself. In all seriousness, tourists like me, are essentially ambassadors for their country so we should try and leave a good impression. Well, perhaps not in France, but elsewhere.

I decided to buy some clothes as people were starting to get too familiar with my suede jacket and my underpants just couldn't take many more washings out in the sink. Like Florida, and indeed, Essex, they have the largest shopping mall in the world so I took the ship's bus there. It's great fun shopping in America and the prices are marvellous. Everything beginning with c is particularly cheap: cigars, cds, cassette players, scent. There's a shop that sells only one product, glasses that play music…no, not drinking glasses, glasses glasses!

I spotted the sign that screamed: ***Nathan's the world's finest dog,*** just like it is in all the books so I nipped across and got in line. What a disappointment! An insipid sausage in a limp roll: 'Help yourself to onions pal,' the man bawled pointing proudly to a sad bowl of chopped Spanish. I mean, what is the point of a hot dog without fried onions? I rest my case. I cheered myself up with a pretzel.

I tried to buy a bow tie from this boutique and was quoted $80. 'It's just been flown in from Italy,' the man explained. 'Well, it must have come first class,' said I. I went in this cheap clothes store for some cheap clothes then stood in the queue for the rest of the day to pay for them. But even this had its compensations, the lady behind me got divorced by phone. Truly! She started by leaving a pertinent message on his voicemail: 'Who were you with last night?' He phoned back, brief bell, book and candle job! Then she finally brought the solemn contract where she promised to love, honour and obey to a close with the words: 'Well, I'll bring around your Christmas present then that's it you smug bugger.' I quickly wrote down the smug bugger bit on my sleeve to try out later on a German. Next, she phoned her attorney and was just talking about what he made her do with a cheese grater and a roll of tin foil when, dammit, I reached the front of the queue. I shan't sleep now, I mean, how many untoward actions can you get up to with a cheese grater and a roll of tin foil?

Well, after my exertions I felt it was time to have a drink, so I looked around and found a peaceful looking bar to have a short rest.

The Purser looked up from his desk a weary expression on his face, 'Are you all right, Dr Walker?' he asked.

'I'm fine, thank you,' said I, 'I had a good day, did some shopping, had a hot dog, then found out something I didn't know before.'

'And, what was that?'

'Handcuffs are cold,' I said. 'Really, they are…you see 'em in the movies slapped on peoples' wrists anyhow, you never stop to consider what temperature they are…do I owe you any money for bail or anything?'

'No, they decided to drop all charges.'

'Ah,' I nodded sagely, 'you know, I had a suspicion that might happen. Well, I'm off for a late supper…thanks for your help.'

'That's okay, Dr Walker,' said the purser, then as I turned to the door, 'Dr Walker?'

'Adsum.'

'It's Jamaica, the day after tomorrow.'

'Yes, I know, cigars, sugar cane, sultry maidens.'

'You will be careful in Jamaica won't you, Dr Walker?'

'Absolutely.' I gave his troubled face a friendly wink, 'I mean what could possibly happen there?'

Paula put down the plate of salad in front of me, 'The sous chef did that special,' she said sitting opposite, 'it's got caviar in it.'

'We thought you could do with a bit of luxury after your Midnight Express experience,' said Daniella who was sitting to the side.

'Yes,' I said wiping my brow, 'it was a terrible ordeal.' I nodded sagely, 'Imagine a hot dog without fried onions!'

'Well?' said Paula, helping herself to a piece of toast and dipping it in my caviar. 'Let's hear it.'

I sighed, 'Well, I went for a drink see?'

'You?' demanded Daniella. 'You don't drink…you can't drink! I've never known anybody with a weaker head, one glass of cider and you're anybody's!'

'Now, be fair, Daniella,' said Paula, 'he's anybody's without the glass of cider.'

'Well, yes, admittedly, my head isn't the strongest when it comes to alcohol,' I said, 'but it rather seemed the thing to do, you know when you're in New York, go in a bar and order a Bourbon.'

'What exactly is Bourbon?' asked Paula getting right to the point.

'I dunno, I never got to find out,' I said. 'I'd just got it when this large man pushed a plate in my face and demanded some money for what he called the freedom fighters in Northern Ireland.'

'Ah,' said Paula, 'so what did you do?'

'I told him a bit bruskly to go away.'

'Yeah, I bet,' said Daniella. She repeated the word bruskly to herself a couple of times.

'Well, he wouldn't go away and he kept on shouting at me in a most offensive manner so I gave him a bit of a push and he fell over a chair and started to cry.'

'So who called the police?' asked Daniella.

'He did,' I said, 'he was the police.'

'Oh shit,' said Paula eruditely, she was trying not to laugh. 'So, what happened?'

'Well, I was sort of sitting there, minding my own business examining my Bourbon, when there was this terrible kerfuffle and suddenly there was this bloody great gun stuffed in my face and I was being dragged off by about five gorillas…I didn't even get to tip the barman, very rude.'

'Did they handcuff you?' demanded Daniella, delightedly.

'You bet they did, handcuffs, hand on head, frantic ride through New York, frog march into the station, the lot' I said.

'Didn't you try to explain?' asked Paula.

'No, I seemed to upset them when they were putting the handcuffs on, so I kept quiet after that,' I said.

'What did you say?' asked Daniella.

'I told them that I usually liked my handcuffs a bit tighter than that.' The two girls looked at each other and sighed.

'Anyway, it was all a blur, lots of people shouting and pushing me then all of a sudden I was standing in this room and there was this man in a white coat putting on a rubber glove in a sort of meaningful way.'

'Oh, they didn't?' gasped Paula.

'Oh, they certainly did,' said I. 'I think you're laughing Paula?'

'No, no,' she said but lost control and sat there tears pouring down her face. Daniella had already gone and was lying with her face pillowed in her arms shaking convulsively.

'It wasn't so funny,' I said, 'when he dunks his hand in that big jar of Vaseline…well, I'm telling you, your whole life flashes in front of your eyes!' This started them off again and I sat there staring reproachfully at my two Jobian comforters.

'It's a funny thing,' I said after a minute, 'but I got talking to the guard afterwards, when I was sort of walking it off…' I paused briefly as Daniella let out another despairing howl, '…I asked him what kind of person applied to do that job.'

'You did?' said Paula wiping her eyes.

'Yeah. And he said they had to be very careful, they had to select very special people. I said, you mean people with thin fingers? And he said no…no, they had to make sure they didn't get anybody who wanted to do the job for the wrong reasons.'

'The wrong reasons?' Paula demanded. 'What would the wrong reasons be for wanting to stick your hand up people's bums for a living?'

'He said they didn't want to risk getting anybody who would enjoy doing it.'

'You mean people would enjoy doing that?' asked Paula.

'Well, exactly,' I said. 'I mean, leaving aside the fact that his using the words **select very special people to do the job** indicates that there was a fair few to choose from, I would have thought that if they have to employ people to do such a job then it would behove them to find someone who got some enjoyment out of it, however vicarious.'

'Oh please stop,' Daniella waved frantically at me, 'I can't take anymore.'

I glared around at them indignantly, 'Anyway, what did they imagine I had up there in the first place? I mean, I didn't know I was going to be arrested did I?'

'I think it's in case you've got a knife…' Paula broke off, then continued in a rush, '…well, in situ, as it were.'

'Well, pardon me for being pedantic, but if I imagined that I was about to get into a knife fight then up my bottom is not the first place that would spring to mind when I was deciding on a place of concealment…I mean it's not exactly a position that lends itself to a fast draw is it?'

Paula had finally given up and had joined Daniella in a heap on the table. I put the last piece of salad in my mouth then rose with as much dignity as I could muster.

'Well, I'm happy to see that my day has kept you amused as usual. Now, if you will excuse me, I will retire to my bed.' I gave the two girls my most portentous look, (I've been practising it in the mirror), 'And I'm trusting you two ladies to see that this doesn't go any further.'

6) Jamaica

The great thing about Jamaica is that it's so friendly. Everybody kept telling me that, and when you meet the Jamaicans themselves they are vehement, up to the point of aggressive, about it being the friendliest island in the Caribbean. I was secretly looking forward to it, half of the James Bond books are set here and I had wanted to visit since I read the rude bits of ***Thunderball*** under the bedclothes when I was seven. I kept looking for the bits Ian Fleming wrote about but we didn't find those exact ones, our tour was more of a urban breakdown and environmental devastation experience.

It was actually called the **Highlights Tour**: We were driven out to the pretty part of the island to view the ravaged trees and (wait for it) sugar cane! We all gasped at the sight, well, I know I did. We got out and broke some off and tried to eat it, guess what, it's like chewing sweet, wet wood…just like a lolly stick in fact. Next we stopped at a wooden shack, I thought it was because someone needed to relieve themselves, but no, it was a café where we were issued with a complimentary glass of Jamaican grapefruit juice. It must be true when people tell me I'm a cynic (or from the Poison Dwarf: a sour faced cynic) because although everybody told us it was fresh local juice: the guide, the driver, the barman, I just couldn't totally believe it especially when he unashamedly poured it straight into the glasses from a cardboard carton with the juice squeezer's name still on it…evidently the man from Del Monte had said yes. Then onto a craft market where we were offered a vast cornucopia of souvenirs to buy of wooden carvings and table mats. This one particularly friendly Jamaican kindly followed me around for a solid quarter of an hour trying to sell me a stuffed snake, I finally stopped, and drawing on my experiences with the New York police, I offered to show him somewhere he could keep it warm. We stopped for photographs and I searched around before deciding to take one of the ship to rivet everybody back home.

    Finally we were left for an hour's shopping on our own. We had a lecture from the Cunard rep on the dangers of wandering away from our four allotted shops which were patrolled by about as many policeman as you see at the Notting Hill Carnival. Then at last our bodyguard, who was a skinny child of about fifteen, let us off the leash. Well, after you've bought some coffee and been horrified at the price of Cuban cigars (I used to smoke them when I ran a tough pub…you'd have to be Branson to do it nowadays), you've about shot your bolt and anyway I was convinced that the fifteen year was rather over egging the pudding. So off I trolled down the main street. It was fine, there was a great big Christmas tree and everybody kept waving strings of beads at me and apart from the poverty of everybody I felt more at home than in Brentwood. In fact when this friendly youth joined me I was a bit put out, especially when he introduced himself as yet someone else working for Cunard, but he was an easy going amiable youth so I agreed to let him give me a tour. He did too, a very good one, he showed me all the exciting shops and the places where they are obviously still rebuilding after the war…funny thing, I hadn't realised that the Second World War had come this far, like they say: travel broadens the mind. After about half an hour I told him I should be getting back and he said he'd take me only he'd show me the oldest church in Jamaica on the way and I didn't want to hurt his feelings so I pretended to take a photograph of this heap of stones and all of a sudden I realised I was off the main road.

Then, two youths came out of the bushes, obviously they were friends of his wanting to meet his new acquaintance, any friend of mine etc. And, it is true they lived up to the Jamaican culture by being especially friendly. One of them came and stood so close I could smell his feet and he produced a flat tin, amazingly it was one of those tins Cadbury's used to issue to school kids…you remember the ones, you had to write an essay then you all got a prize? Anyway, I was pleased to see that he too had evidently written a Cadbury's essay, to be honest, I was pleased to garner evidence that he had actually been in a school because these second two lacked the sartorial elegance of my guide. He opened the box but disappointingly the chocolates had long gone and all that was in there was a rusty knife.

'Hand it over, we don't want to have to have to cut you,' said the third youth through a most intriguing set of broken teeth.

'Make it $100,' said the Cadbury's man, 'or I'm going to have to use it.' My guide all this time was standing there looking slightly embarrassed. Well, I thought, they'd been friendly enough to show me their knife so I took mine out and showed it to them.

'I wouldn't want to cut you either,' I said, taking care to preserve the friendly atmosphere, but even so I could tell it led to ill feeling, my knife was so much nicer than theirs: much bigger and shinier. I leaned against a tree and took out my wallet, 'Look,' I said, taking out the $200

I was still carrying after the inroads of the coffee, 'I must tip my guide here. I was planning on leaving him $20 but as there are three of you I think it would only be polite to leave you $10 each.' I took out the three notes and put my wallet away. I held the notes out towards them but my hands were kinda full what with my big shiny knife and all. 'I am only sorry that I can't afford to pay you $100.' I said. My guide obviously understood my predicament, he had gone a slightly green colour but he took the money after a brief argument with the other two, I have no idea what they were finding to fall out about and was saddened by the lessening of the friendly atmosphere but I guess even the best of friends have their differences.

    My guide then showed me how to get back to the bus but he apparently had a pressing appointment elsewhere because, when I offered to reciprocate, he didn't seem to want to come with me to meet my friends. So, making sure I didn't turn my back on my three new friends, (I have read that in some countries this is considered rude so I wanted to be extra careful), I made my way back to the bus.

    The driver asked me how my tour had gone and I told him about the friendly Jamaicans and he seemed to get very excited about my experiences. Do you know that no less than three of his friends, (all of them policemen), wanted to hear exactly what had happened, they even wrote it down in their notebooks…I expect it's for a radio programme or a newspaper article, something like our *Magic Moments*. And do you know, Jamaica still hadn't finished with its hospitality. Two of the most charming young ladies from the Jamaican embassy were waiting on the quay just to see that I was okay and had had a good day. One of them was truly concerned about my health and seemed to have got in her mind that I might have cut myself somewhere, perhaps it was on all that sugarcane…I really should be more careful. Certainly it was one of those special days that only come once!

7 Bonaire

I don't know how it's happened but everybody seems to know about my experiences with the New York police. It can't be Paula or Daniella which was my first thought because when I broached the subject with them they both denied it. Whatever, the fact remains that a lot of idle amusement is being had at my expense. When I sat down to dinner last night there was a cushion on my chair and the chef did me a special rump steak. At the dance lesson Warren announced that he was going to teach **The**

Black Bottom by popular request, and almost everybody keeps using phrases like: we need to get to the bottom of this or now we've finally bottomed out. Even Big C's at it, during this morning's announcements he mentioned that we might have to stop over in Sydney to have our bottom scraped!

Onto Bonaire (I dunno, somewhere in the Caribbean I expect). I nearly didn't bother going ashore, I felt I'd had all the friendliness I could stand on Jamaica and in New York. And that's something you can't explain, you don't really want to go ashore! I mean, you do go ashore of course, though some of the older people on the World cruise never set foot on dry land from Southampton to Southampton, and it is rumoured that the first mate hasn't been off the ship for eight years. What happens is that you get settled into your nice little routine: dancing, training, eating, swimming, insulting Germans, and it's such an enormous effort to go ashore for what will only turn out to be another disappointment.

Bonny, (that's the sophisticated way to say it), was no exception, another dry, barren island but this time clean and small. I don't want to give you the impression that I am going around wearing my Little Englander shirt, in fact most of the others at my table laugh at me because I keep on defending the locals, but I can only report what I see. But as it turned out, I had a great day. Firstly, I took a stroll around the capital city, which took all of ten minutes. I keep on going in jewellery shops, it's only when I'm inside them and I'm staring around pathetically that I remember I've got no one to buy anything for anymore. I'm also scared of going SCUBA diving, I've never dived on my own. The Poison Dwarf and I learned together and she was the only buddy (diving partner) I ever had but I

brought my diving stuff with me so I braced myself and went and hired this beautiful Dutch girl to take me and it was brilliant. We went straight in off the beach, the water was so warm we didn't even need a wet suit. It didn't have the corals of the Red Sea but there were masses fish, we saw two octopi and Onya, (the Dutch girl), dragged me away from a moray. I think I've laid a ghost there, no, no, no! Not laid in that way.
I staggered back to the ship with my equipment, had dinner, then went to see Des O'Connor. I know I wouldn't see him at home but live he was okay. Anyway, it was this Mexican girl, I'd met her in the pool the day before and she wanted to go, she had formed the impression that Des O'Connor was one of our number one rock stars and nothing I said or he did could dissuade her from this notion. Every time he finished singing **Dick A Dum Dum** or something she'd be on her feet whistling and clapping like she was at an Elvis concert. I kept edging my chair away, I mean it was embarrassing. I finally chickened out in the interval and I offered to fetch her a strawberry ice and never returned. Now I've got to avoid all that side of the ship for a week.

      Anyway, the way to meet women is at the ballroom dance lessons which are held every morning when we're at sea. These are good fun and as every night the main ballroom is packed with women, of all ages literally hungering for a dance partner, then they are required reading (as it were) for the red blooded male. I tried it but garnered nothing, evidently I'm not a good enough dancer just yet. I thought I was doing okay at the lessons until two days ago when I partnered up with a Japanese lady. We went around the floor once, (I was trying to do the Tango…I dunno what she was doing) then she suddenly thrust me savagely away with both arms and shouted out: 'No! No! No!' and dashed away up the passageway, leaving everybody staring at me. I tried an ingratiating smile but it didn't come off and some of the women actually drew their skirts away from me, a thing I have never actually witnessed before in real life...I've been smelling my armpits ever since. Still, I've found my ideal partner, she knows all the dances and doesn't mind waiting for me, she's wonderfully supple and she can avoid my feet whatever they happen to be doing at the time. She's very kind, (I'm into kindness lately, it's an underrated attribute), and she loves dancing with me, so much so that as we circle the dance floor she keeps stroking my back. Her name's Beverley and she's 78, I had a date with her last night and you should have seen us do the Rumba, I think it was me they were cheering.

Beverley is my sort of intro into the super rich society on board and some of them are very rich indeed. Beverley herself is on board for 88 days and has booked a second cabin, next to hers, just to hang 88 dresses in it! One man has on board over 50 suits and 100 shirts. All this has gone towards emphasising a problem I have been having. You'll remember it was the sea trunk that made me come on the cruise? Well, after I had packed that there was very little else I felt I needed so I just brought a couple of suitcases full of books and my SCUBA stuff. The trunk caused a lot of problem, things have obviously changed since the great days of sea travel because they had to take the door off to get it in. I don't think I can have been firing on all cylinders when I packed the trunk because most of the stuff contained in its maw, though endlessly fascinating, is not in the strictest meaning of the term, a fully rounded wardrobe. Please witness, I have: a lava lamp, five small planks of wood, half a pair of Wellington boots, sundry items of catering equipment including a hand mixer, a washing line with clothes pegs, a framed photograph of Lenin's tomb, three lilos, a fan heater, a plastic model of a Sopwith Camel and a tin of Birds Custard. So you can see, though superbly equipped in most ways for a world cruise, I have little in the way of clothing. Still, maybe Beverley will adopt me and get me kitted out like Elton John's toy boy.

8 Curacao

The next day was Curacao and that was the problem: the next day! We needed a day at sea to get back into our routine and give us a chance to bloat out on ship food again. I took a highlights tour of this, nice, and much more built up island. I was, of course, thrilled to be taken around a museum to view the artefacts of the islanders, but interesting as bone fish hooks are I have to admit that after the first fifty the fascination begins to fade. Then onto the liqueur factory. This was marred by the Mexican Des O'Connor fan getting there ahead of us which necessitated me ducking off on my own to hide behind the vats. But my originality was rewarded because I was quickly adopted by a simple-minded Curacaoian who had one tooth. Seriously, just the one but he was so proud of it that he sort of hooked it over his bottom lip so you could see it at all times even when his mouth was closed. He took me on my own private tour, aha I thought, perhaps I'm going to meet some more friendly locals but no he merely gave me a conspiratorial wink, flashed his tooth, then drew off what seemed to be a large flagon of the liqueur. Bloody hell, I don't drink even normal spirits but this stuff was bright blue and smelled like paraffin. It tasted like it as well, he stood there beaming while I was forced to swallow the lot.

It was powerful stuff though, like drinking a glass of embalming fluid but now I feared no foe and sneaked outside and waited behind the refreshment kiosk. Out she came all black hair and flashing eyes, at least she'd stopped applauding, so I walked up to her and presented her with a chocolate ice: 'I'm sorry, they didn't have any strawberry,' I said. She started to thank me brokenly in Spanish but it was going on and on and getting louder and louder so I decided to cut the highlights tour short, you can take only so much pleasure in one day.

    I had a sort of sleep for a couple of hours in this little open car I found until I was woken up by this man shouting at me in the most rude manner. So I went and fetched my SCUBA equipment. There is a major dive centre on the island so I took a taxi and he dropped me in completely the wrong place. I had to carry my dive bag which weighs about as much as a dead body (or a live one come to that) over a mile so I was less than joyful and four inches shorter when I arrived at the reception desk. The girl on reception must be sleeping with the management because she truly didn't know anything, just kept smiling and pointing out the various attractions. I tried telling her that I'd seen everything worth seeing on the highlights tour but this was rewarded with another smile. I only managed to find the dive centre by getting the bloke off ***Information*** to accompany me, he was quite willing to do so, he even let me hold his shoulder in a pincerlike grip until we got there. The receptionist on the new desk then told me I had to go right back to the first desk to get a diving ticket so I told him he was a useless black bastard and stomped off in a rage. I told the Curacaoian who had recommended the dive centre what I thought of him and kicked an inoffensive metal rubbish bin into the sea. Shit! What do they make bins out of on Curacao? Lead? I limped back to my cabin, stripped off my soaking clothes, had a shower and then for some reason I had another little nap on the carpet. I awoke with a splitting headache and took another taxi back to the dive centre and apologised to the man for the black comment: 'I mean, I still think you're a useless bastard but your colour has nothing to do with it...if you were white you'd still be a useless bastard.' I think he got my point but he still didn't seem that happy but I feel it's up to the British to set a standard of behaviour for others to emulate.

I think I must be getting too much sun because my headache was now even worse, in fact the only thing that made it bearable was the excruciating pain in my toe. I decided to try and salvage the day and went to see the film ***Gladiator,*** you know, the one with the unspeakable Antipodean in. It started off okay but then an old lady, sitting in the front row mind you, kept standing up and going through a series of exercises apparently for her back, so I went back to my cabin for a sulk.

Well, we've got a day at sea to recover then it's Bermuda...you know I really think I've broken my toe!

9 Barbados

'Ere listen, it wasn't Bermuda, it was Barbados. Anyway, they're practically the same place so it hardly matters. Big C told me it was Barbados…at 8.30 via the overhead speaker, I mean, that's bad enough, I don't like surfacing before ten, but then they translate the same message into five other languages: 'And now here's our Sonia to give us all the French notices!' And today they went too far: 'And now here's our Yoyo to give us all the Japanese notices!' Have you noticed when they give the announcement in another language it's always a lot longer than it was in English? You get this feeling that they are saying something extra for them, or maybe something rude about us! Anyway, after the Japanese fiasco I climbed up on the bed and got at the speaker with me Swiss army penknife and silenced it forever.

    I was coming down the main stairs for a late breakfast when I came upon the whole Japanese contingent having their group photograph taken so I naturally got on the back. The two Japs either side of me expressed surprise at first, then they jabbered at one another and in unison each linked an arm around my shoulders and turned their flashing teeth back to the camera. I must say I've come out awfully well.

    The QE2 is magnificent, it has to be lived to be believed: the glamour, the elegance, the food, the friendliness of the staff…the sheer scale of everything! But the single thing that must stick in everybody's mind is the afternoon tea. On any day hundreds of passengers can be found lurking around the main lounge, innocent smiles stitched across their faces but it's the smile of the tiger for the second 4 o clock strikes they turn into a rampaging hoard and in a kind of restrained mad rush they make for the seats. It's the QE2 so there isn't any actual fist fighting, you understand, but more a sort of polite nudging of your competitors with your bottom if they attempt to get into your favourite seat. Then, as we all sit glaring at the serving doors saliva running down our chins, the lady harpist strikes up, funny, you don't really listen to a harp do you? You cannot imagine queuing up for a harp concert, but here she fits in perfectly, besides which, you're not here to listen you're here for the food! I think she's really there to cover up the sound of frantically working jaws. Then the doors open and two never ending lines of waiters and waitresses appear bearing silver trays aloft. Firstly they serve you your hot drink of choice, all done with immaculate Cunard style, then the sandwiches come out: a huge silver tray is offered to you with row after row of tiny sandwiches containing every filling known to man and you just help yourself to row after row of them, and then just when you cannot eat anything more without actually dying the tray is there again. And still it goes on, you sit back in your chair panting for breath and the lines of waiters and waitresses start up again and this time the silver tray is covered with cakes, and cakes…and cakes! Unbelievable, there can be anything up to twenty different cakes on a tray and here's the wonderful thing: they are all tiny so you can have dozens of them, and then more dozens. There is one enormously fat man, I shall call him Stanley, who cries when he is urged to choose, he sits there tears dribbling down his face, selecting yet another row of cakes…it's not the prettiest of sights. Then ponderously, gaseously and very, very slowly we all stagger off to bed to sleep it all off in time for dinner.

I've had to limit myself to one afternoon tea a week or I'd never get down the gangplank. Instead I go and swim four hundred lengths of the swimming pool while the rest of them are eating. This is not as impressive as it sounds as it's the indoor pool, (I'm never witnessed outside), and it's a bit small, four hundred lengths is about a mile but still impressive to the rest of them on board. I managed to fall out with a woman in the pool yesterday, and surprise, surprise, she was German. She summoned me to the side with an imperious finger and informed me that she only ever swam circuits and furthermore she had a bad leg so I was to make sure I stayed out of her way. I told her that she was out of luck because I, as well as everybody else on the ship, only swam lengths, and furthermore my greatest wish was to stay out of her way at every possible opportunity. She started shouting at me in German so I told her to go and invade Poland and she goose-stepped off in a huff. She went and filled in a letter of complaint about me but it backfired because the sports director is a mate of mine and she was issued with a formal communication asking that, for the sake of the other passengers, would she please care to swim lengths for the duration.

The sports director? Well, he's called Mike and I've got to know him quite well. I weight train in the gym every morning we're at sea and obviously there is very little competition so I seem like Arnold here, old ladies keep coming up to me and saying I'm very brave. Then I go to the adjoining workout room and practice karate for an hour and this gets another small, but dedicated, audience. Mike, who doesn't know a great deal about lifting, and nothing about karate, got interested and started asking bits of advice, and then I managed to cure his rotator cuff injury, something that has been troubling him for years.

Another thing that's working well for me is I'm learning to use the computer. What happened was this: the Poison Dwarf wanted a new computer so I took her into Chelmsford and bought her one. She had got talking to the man while I had been wandering around trying not to scream with boredom, and he had shown her this brand new, top of the range, Sony laptop that a had just been delivered. It was out of our price-range, (shit, it was out of everybody's price range), and anyway she was after a desktop but she fell in love with thing and didn't stop talking about it for weeks. When she asked me to leave I nipped into Chelmsford and bought one just to piss her off…and boy, did it! It was worth all the money I wasted.

I brought the damned thing on board with me and decided it was time I began to keep up with the times so I lugged it down to the bar with me. It took me two days just to open the damned thing and switch it on but then I'd stop any passing person under the age of thirty and ask them how to do things, like write a letter, save a letter, erase a letter…switch it off. Now a month later and I can just about work it, I'm writing all this stuff on it and it's got to be said that the spellchecker is a marvel!

Well, then, Barbados: not a bad little island, very friendly people, very British. It's a typical Caribbean island with a clean capital city and lots of poverty outside. There's a lot of traffic, in fact, congestion is a real problem here. I went into Bridgetown and wandered around for an hour and bought a wonderful set of Christmas tree lights for half price. The tourist information fixed me up with a dive so I fetched my stuff and took a taxi. It wasn't exactly state-of-the-art, I was the most experienced diver there for

Heaven's sake except for the dive master and he was German so doesn't count. I was buddied up with an American doctor who was very nervous and asked me to keep an eye on him but he lost faith in me when I couldn't get under the water. I had forgotten that when I dived in Bonaire I hadn't worn a wet suit and a suit makes you over 2 kilos lighter in the water. In the end the German had to fetch me more weight from his car, he was well pleased to de-suit and trudge back up the beach while we all waited in the searing heat.

The dive was okay but more barren that Bonaire, there were lots of wrecks but the fish were hiding and the water wasn't that clear. It was the first time I've dived from a small boat with a backward entry and the removal of your gear before you exit, it was in the bay and an enjoyable new experience. Then came the interminable drive back to the ship by a tone-deaf reggae fan, I was glad I still had water in my ears. Then I went and hired a Harley and went for a blaze around the island. There were a few nice beaches and a classic English telephone box and then some sort of snake sanctuary to look around. I came to a deal with the guide that I'd pay him the going rate if he'd leave me alone. But the best thing about Barbados was the sign I discovered high in the hills, it was advertising a dentist and read: ***Tooth extraction $1…with gas $10!***

I was absolutely delighted to find that the electricity supply in my cabin matches my new lights so I immediately decorated the place with one thousand brightly flashing bulbs. It's a funny thing but ever since I did so my cabin steward, Lito, has started treating me with a kind of understanding delicacy.

10 St Thomas

I bought a painting at the art auction and yes, it just happens to be a painting of a pretty lady with a bare bottom. The bare bottom was purely incidental I bought it for the chiaroscuro. I don't know where I got this reputation from, every time they put a painting up of a pretty lady Paula looks over at me and says: 'We'll ask Dr Walker to open the bidding on this one.' She started one nude off at £200 and glanced over at me, I said I could get a real one for that. Then I offered to bid if she would deliver it personally to my cabin. Oh all right, chiaroscuro means the contrast between black and white!

St Thomas is one of the Virgin Islands, there's nothing I can say to that. It's very pretty and the bay is lovely. We had to moor offshore so I stayed in bed until all the tours had gone then caught the tender. One of the crew asked me for a queuing ticket and barred my way, I sort of gave him a look and he quickly stood aside and wished me a nice day. I don't go a bundle on his chances if a band of Somalian pirates tries to board us.

We landed at the main town which consists of one grocers, a massage parlour and 3 million jewellers, (I'm still going in them!). They don't seem to SCUBA dive and no one will hire you a motorbike: 'They're too dangerous, sir,' so I rented a car and went for a tour. That's the only real complaint I have about this cruise, the constant nurse-maiding: you can't hire a motorbike, they won't recommend dive sites, put your foot here as you get off the tender…actually, they have stopped saying this last to me since I told the gangplank man what I was thinking of doing with my foot, back in Florida. Do you know they even have young girls offering to carry your tray for you in the Lido in case you fall and hurt yourself? And yes, she refused to carry it as far as my cabin.

I finally found the beach and wandered along it to where my group were all sunbathing: Paula, Dorcus and Daniella. Daniella's husband was there as well but he was off doing some Adonis thing with a beach ball and two beach bunnies. I was a little taken aback to find that all three of the girls were topless and they found this hugely funny, it was only then they revealed that it was a nudist beach. Now, I know that along with the best of people, I'm fond of mooning when the occasion calls for it, but in cold blood? Anyway, purely from an artistic point of view, I elected to keep my shorts firmly on. It is surprising, however, just how difficult it is to play really effective volley ball with three, gorgeous, semi-nude women.

We got back well in time for dinner and it's all getting too much. Remember me asking the maitre de to fill my table with young nubile women? Well, he's still taking the piss! Last night we had an addition to replace the late, unlamented Sid. We got Earnest. Earnest is 92, he's both half blind and half deaf, partially crippled and has just lost his wife of 60 years, so he's a real bundle of laughs. It's a pity my cheering section doesn't eat dinner but Dorcus and Daniella are staff and Paula only eats at lunchtime.

The main thing that is bothering me, though, is this business of the person in the next cabin. I've worked out that he's a Scotsman from the fact he spends over an hour every evening tossing a caber around his cabin, nothing else could explain the row. He's young too, because he plays loud rock music at every hour of the day or night, I quite like it. And he obviously bought a new set of bongos in Barbados because he's been accompanying the rock music on them, I am less fond of that. I finally bumped into him last night for the first time, he's a very old man who uses two of those walking sticks with clawed feet to get around…what's going on?

I was invited to the Captain's party last night, don't be too impressed, everybody gets at least one invite. You all queue up to have the honour of shaking his hand, I was enormously eager to do this, after all whenever I use a bus I make a point of going around to the side door and shaking the bus driver's hand. Well, after waiting nearly half an hour, the great moment arrived and I strode forward in eager anticipation for this memorable meeting. He grabbed my hand and gave me the Maggie Thatcher pull past, or tried to, sadly for him I am stronger than he is (all that weight training), and he ended up against the passageway wall. I told him that if he didn't want to bother speaking to me he should omit me from the invite list from here on and went off in a bit of a huff…I do find that so rude.

I was scowling at the other partygoers when a voice said: 'Wow, you look in a good mood.' 'I've just fallen out with the driver,' said I, taking the glass of champagne Paula was offering. She grinned, 'I always come in from behind the curtains,' she nodded to the stage, 'that way you don't have all that bloody queuing…tell you what, come and have some caviar.'

Have I told you about caviar? Well, the QE2 uses up half of the world's supply. Half of the world's supply! And it's not the most expensive thing on their shopping list, that distinction belongs to saffron (the Captain's quiz, day one icebreaker). It's served all the time in the top dining rooms, the boring ones, and some people have it 3 times a day. One couple even asks for caviar sandwiches when they go ashore. What you do is this: you accept a plate from the steward, a good plate too, considering, I feel if they cut down the size of the plates, (and the number of sandwiches), then it might go down to a quarter of the world's supply. Anyway, your plate contains a number of triangles of burnt toast and a pile of glistening black beads. You heap some of the beads onto a piece of toast, squeeze lemon juice over it, put a spoonful of grated onion on the top then drape it all in a mound of crumbled boiled egg. You then pop it in and chew it slowly, and if you're a sophisticate you swallow it with you eyes closed in a kind of dreamy euphoria. What does it taste like? Exactly like burnt toast with lemon, onion and crumbled boiled egg!

I must have still been feeling miffed because I did something enormously outrageous last night, let me set the scene: every article of clothing you buy in America immediately starts shedding its buttons like Japanese cherry blossoms in a typhoon. I seem to spend every evening sewing them back on again, (I did ask Arletta at my table to help but she just collapsed into gales of laughter). Well, my dinner jacket lost both of its main buttons and you just can't find anything quite that size to replace them. Next, let me introduce you to MIKE! It's always said like that in capital letters: MIKE! I don't like MIKE. He's the kid at school you used to beat up for no real reason, he's got a big fat, flabby face and a loud whining voice, the only comparison I can come up with is it sounds like a hyena being slowly squashed by a steamroller…and he's always there, you know! The final part of this drama is that if you want anything cleaning (and if you are a millionaire), you hang it on a hook outside your door--aha! Well, MIKE left his dinner jacket out last night so at 3 o clock I nipped up the passageway and snipped the buttons off. I took the lot: the pretentious three down the front, the ones on the sleeves, even the two spares. There's been ever such a kerfuffle. I'm writing this in my normal place at the front of the art auction waiting for it to start. I always spend this hour writing on my computer. I can hear MIKE ranting on about his jacket still, I stopped on my way past and told him how awful it was and he thanked me. They all think that I'm working on a book so they keep a respectful distance but I'm really sitting here gloating over MIKE'S jacket…ha ha!

I've lately become part of the art auction. What happened is this: Paula used to employ the baker from the kitchens to put the paintings up for her as she auctioned them. Well, he fell out with his assistant, it turned very physical when the assistant threw a French loaf at him…it acted like a spear and caught him in the eye. The baker is a big lad, and very hot tempered so he grabbed the assistant, forced him into one of the huge ovens, locked it, and was trying to light the gas when he was restrained by four other chefs. At the enquiry it was decided that he was too valuable to loose, (his scones have to be tasted to be believed), but that he wasn't to be trusted with any of the passengers. A strange decision you might feel, but when you think about it more deeply, quite reasonable: it might just be acceptable to bake up an assistant chef in an oven but it would bound to make the front pages if he did it to say a millionaire banker from Boston.

So, Paula lost her assistant and I stepped in **pro tem** and it worked so well that she kept me on, though I insisted on working without pay. It's good fun, whenever there's a lull I keep putting up nudes and every time she turns around there is another monstrous pair of tits looking at her. My big success came, though, with the cartoon sale.

Believe it or not the biggest auction of the week is when she auctions off the original cartoons done by Hanna Barbara. These things fetch hundreds, sometimes, thousands of pounds…did you know that their originality is guaranteed? Hanna Barbara mixed their blood in with the ink they used to sign the drawings so the DNA can be checked. Back to the auction: I can impersonate many of the Disney cartoons so when I put up say, Donald Duck I would protest in his voice: **'No I'm not going up there…the other way up idiot…I'm not being sold for that!'** That sort of thing. We had the crowd in fits, even Paula couldn't speak for laughing…I think I've found a new career: cartoon animal impersonator!

    Well, well, well, I had a bust up last night in the movie theatre and guess what nationality they were? Here's a hint: they like sausages! It was ***Shakespeare in Love*** and as usual I made my way to my accustomed seat so my back is against the wall. I like sitting there because I can fidget and scratch myself to my heart's content without fear of upsetting anyone behind. The theatre wasn't busy, about 30 people, so this couple refused to let me past and this vile woman snarled at me and told me to find somewhere else to sit. I told her that her cruise ticket didn't give her ownership of the whole boat and pushed past. Now I will admit that I didn't go to any great lengths to avoid their feet but I truly didn't see her drink. I sat down and made myself comfy while they stood up and howled abuse at me. After a while I asked them whether they enjoyed the sound of their own voices and assured them nobody else did, a view which the whole audience loudly shared as by this time the movie had started. She was going on like she was wound up and I couldn't concentrate on the movie so I wandered over, ignored her, and asked him conspiratorially why he didn't take her up to the boat deck and shove her over the side—this got a round of applause from the four people sitting in front who were also trying to watch the movie. He shook his fist at me, I gave him a Hitler salute then tried the only German phrase I know out on him: 'Du bist ein grosse pimmel.' I think it means something like: *you are an enormous male member.* It certainly means something rude because they kinda sank back in their seats into stunned oblivion and after a few minutes of peace they slunk out…and yes, I enjoyed the movie enormously.

11 Columbia

I've got a job! I don't get paid or anything but it saves me money and that's all to the good because when I get home, well it'd be better to say when I get back to Britain because I no longer have a home, I'll be flat broke. What happened is this, the next stop is Columbia and we've been warned about Columbia. It's a dangerous country and you shouldn't go around on your own which is a bit hard if you don't fancy any of the tours and hell, would you? The folklore of Columbia. A tour of the coffee plantations. A trip to see the grand houses of Columbia with musical interludes for your enjoyment!

I had been intending to go round for a stroll on my own but the day before a note was delivered to my cabin asking me to visit one of the cabins on the quarterdeck, (very rich). I thought it was the two sausage eaters from the movie wanting to intimidate me with their money so I sent a note back saying if they wanted to speak to me to make sure they were at my cabin at 4 o clock. Bang on 4 a middle-aged lady turned up and she told me that she and her husband wanted to hire a car to see the sights and they wondered whether I would consider going with them. It appeared they had asked at the purser's office whether there was a member of the crew who they could employ as a bodyguard and the purser had recommended they have a word with me, I suppose it's after that misunderstanding in Jamaica. They wanted someone who would deal with all the taxi drivers and shoo off the street traders, that sort of thing. It sounded a bit of a laugh so I said yes, only I wouldn't accept any money and would like a say in where we went.

    At ten the following morning I wandered off the ship to find a gleaming limousine waiting at the quayside, air-conditioned with a uniformed chauffeur, and get this, a local lady schoolteacher, hired for the day as a guide. I had a good day, it was much better than going around on my own and I didn't pay for anything. The couple were called June and John, (sounds a bit like a nursery rhyme), and they were from Poole where they have an agricultural business, I have no idea what that means. Anyway, the car would take us somewhere, the teacher would give us a (thank Heavens) short talk, then the chauffeur would get out and announce in ringing tones that these were very important people who had to have their own bodyguard. Well, I think that's what he said but the only words I understood were SAS so I feel he was prone to exaggeration. I would climb out trying to look tough, giving a bit of a sniff at everybody and eyeing them up and down and it was amazing, everybody backed away, imagine anybody being scared of me. It worked best in the shops, the good shops all have armed guards on the doors and these automatically accepted me as a compatriot. They would show me their rifles (Armalites) and their CS gas canisters and I would nod knowledgably. Inside the shops I would get offered ice cold cans of beer and when I would turn these down and ask for Coke they would all jabber away approvingly at my professionalism. In one shop the guard commander immediately went around knocking the beer cans out of his men's hands after he had met me. I got given a tiny emerald in one shop for taking June and John there and in another a piece of rock with the emeralds still in it. We saw just about everywhere and what a pretty place it is, much better than any of the Caribbean islands, it's all Spanish-type villas and balconies with bright colours everywhere. The architecture is good and the walled city fascinating, it is an ancient fort from 400 odd years ago. The traders are fun, I only had to frighten one belt seller off and he was reasonably cheerful about it. Another of them kept trying to sell me a genuine Rolex watch for $75, to get rid of him I offered $10 and it was hilarious, he kept appearing at intervals and the price kept getting less and less. I stuck to my $10. I don't know how he kept finding us but wherever we went he kept popping up: 'Sah, you pay $35 for this good watch.' Finally at the end of the day he was waiting at the quayside for us and he handed me the watch and asked for the $10! Imagine that a Rolex watch for $10! It must be genuine, he swore on the soul of his dead mother that it was!

  We went to the Hilton for coffee and that's where I really learned about June and John. I ordered one of those tiny, very strong, black coffees and they were quite happy with that but when it came to choosing something for themselves, oh shit! They must have gone down that damned menu 20 times asking how big each drink was, analysing the prices. In the end, after they had argued about the different prices of bottled water for at least 10 minutes, the waitress, (she was an American girl), said, 'Oh listen, I'll pay it for you.' And they thought that was a result! I bought some coffee and vanilla as recommended, they examined some for 20 minutes then decided not to. In fact they looked at everything in the bloody town and decided not to buy anything as the day progressed. Oh the jewellery she got them to show her, the clothes she made them strip of manikins before walking away, the bits of cheese and wine he tasted! Then at last we made it to the jewellery factory and as June started her usual nonsense John and I were shown how they mined the stones and turned them into jewellery, fascinating. Then John approached me holding the biggest damned emerald you have ever seen, it looked like a bird's egg! He told me he wanted to buy it and they wanted $17,000 for it and did I think I could get it for any less? Just watch me. One outraged glare got it down to $14,000 and after another half an hour's shouting it had come down to $12,000, and there it stuck. John kept wanting to accept and I had all but to clap a hand over his mouth. I ordered June and John out into the waiting car, the engine was actually going when, of course, they came running out after us. Finally, I brokered a deal, they would accept $10,000 in the form of a cheque, no cards and it would be an open cheque so they could fiddle the tax and they would follow us back to the QE2 to fetch it. We were sitting in the car, the stone, now in the form of a necklace, all wrapped up, when bloody June changes her mind. It took all my reassurances, (she wouldn't listen to John at all, after all he was only paying for the sodding thing), to get her to realise what a bargain she had got.

Anyway, they were ecstatic about my help and asked me what I was doing in Costa Rica, well, I'll have to see, they were fine to me but so mean to everybody else—do you know they messed the poor chauffeur around rotten and kept him 2 hours longer than he was hired for but when it came time to pay him they counted out his money to the penny. I felt so ashamed I slipped him $20.

I am very happy with my watch though. Do you know if you shake it hard it starts to run backwards? Wow! All that for just $10.

12 Costa Rica

We are going through the Panama Canal today to get to Costa Rica. Here's some interesting facts: it costs over £150,000 to take the QE2 through the canal! It costs over £10,000 an hour just to dock at New York but the most expensive place to dock in the whole world is Southampton: £15,000 per hour! You can see that can't you, everybody wants to visit sunny Southampton.

It takes all day to go through the canal and an impressive structure it is, it actually joins a number of big lakes up so at times you can hardly see the sides but at others there are literally only inches each side to spare and Big C must be scraping the paint off all the way. There are dozens of liners using it at any one time and we followed our sister ship, Coronia, through and the Captains kept on hooting at one another…with the ship's hooters I mean. Yes, it is certainly impressive, but attractive? No! I soon crept back below to the air conditioning because that's where the cruise is happening.

I think the ship is great. The service is wonderful and the food terrific. I don't know how they ever make a profit. I found a big ice cream machine screwed to the wall by the swimming pool, it serves four flavours and you just go up and help yourself and it's all free. Some people aboard seem to live on this ice cream and are rarely found more than 100 feet from the magic machine.

Then there's the boardroom. They've opened this up as a private room for people who are on the world cruise but the real reason you go in it is because all the other Plebs can't: ha ha! They have a lady butler called Yoyo and any number of stewards to look after your every want, they will literally get you anything from a boiled egg to a piano. I just jokingly said to Yoyo that they hadn't got me a desk to write at and the next day when I went in there it was...now I've got to go in even when I don't want to!

I like Yoyo, she is a stunningly attractive Japanese girl but after sitting one afternoon, writing at my desk in earshot I can forgive her even that. She had a phone call from her boyfriend who is one of the chefs (my cheering section know everything) it seemed they hadn't been ashore together for weeks so they arranged to have a meal in Costa Rica at this posh restaurant he loves. Next in comes Guy. Now Guy is this cadaverous American with a loud and very annoying, penetrating voice, but you have to like him because Guy is blind. He gets Yoyo to book a table for him at the same restaurant and then asks her, Yoyo, whether she would consider accompanying him. Without a pause she agreed in a delighted voice that made me feel warm inside and then I had to listen to her attempting to explain to her boyfriend why she was going to his restaurant with someone else...as I said, I like Yoyo!

And now I come to the research project I am undertaking. After all as a scientist I feel to waste such a wonderful opportunity as a world cruise to do some serious study would be a sin. After all, Darwin didn't waste his journey at sea, he spent it writing one of the greatest fairy stories of all time. The conundrum was, what to study. Well, ever since I started wearing contact lenses and I learned to see, two things have fascinated me: firstly, there's trees. The sheer diversity of them (I thought they were all fir) the different leaf shapes, the myriad fruits, the nuts, the differing ways the branches hang, the colours, the colours and again the colours, these are things I didn't know existed. The second thing is the large amount of women walking around with enormous breasts. Consequently, I have opted to study the latter. This is pure science because although liking all women (except for Germans of course) it is not necessarily the women who are blessed in this way that I lean towards.

I have observed that women in Britain with large breasts tend to apologise for them, they walk around with their arms folded across their chests as though they can hide them from public view. They squeeze into lifts, holding themselves in and murmuring apologies as they go as though it is somehow their fault…I somehow can't imagine Errol Flynn apologising for anything untowardly huge that he possessed! In the US it is entirely different. If you have large breasts in America you wear something tight to exaggerate them, then you hoist them up and steam forward like a battleship demanding people give you extra room. 'Look at me,' you are proclaiming, 'I've got enormous tits!'. In California it's against the law to have small breasts, if you are a woman that is. People will actually tell you about it and offer you the phone number of their plastic surgeon. Some women will even get aggressive about it: 'So what's wrong with you then? Can't you afford the operation or are you scared?' While in California I was briefly enrolled in an exhilaratingly embarrassing conversation between the lady I was with and a total stranger about where the erogenous zones were once the plastic surgeon had had his evil way…I slipped away when they both started rolling up their blouses as the conversation reached the hands-on point.

Caribbean women come in two types, and only two: the adorable, slim virgins (sic) with their coltish limbs and almond Renoir eyes (hang on my glasses have started to fog up). Once these girls are married they immediately turn into the second type, the great big, fat, jolly women with booming laughs, you see at the Notting Hill Carnival trying on policeman's helmets. You never see them in the in-between stage, I think they must have fattening sheds like the Masai people in Africa where they send young brides to turn them into baby-making factories.

Anyway, for the purposes of research it is the latter group of ladies who are more interesting for Caribbean women do not use their breasts as sex objects, or even prestige, but as a tool. They push themselves through crowds with them and somehow being hurled aside by a massive mammary doesn't seem to engender the same aggressive response in the victim as say a shoulder produces. Instead everybody chuckles and shouts out things like: 'Hey there big Momma,' and, 'Make room for all three of them.' These ladies use them to carry shopping, to display goods for sale, as levers to lift heavy objects and to shut cupboards and doors. In (friendly) Jamaica our ship's guide was struggling to close the bus door when our massive Jamaican guide came waddling up booming with laughter, bunted him out the way with a quick tit jab, then with a cataclysmic swing of her hips she crashed the door shut with a great thrust of breasts…amazing! I even met one lady in Bonaire who used hers to point with when giving directions. I wanted to ask her the directions to two places in opposite directions to see how she would cope but lost my nerve at the last moment.

Incidentally, I did witness on Bonaire, something I have only read about in the past. The men have a kind of parallel behaviour, pale and insipid though it may be in the face of their women's proclivities: they point the way with their lips! Still, I suppose it is better than pointing with other parts of their anatomy, and more reliable.

I've got my own place in the Lido where I work at night, my own chair and everything. It's a good place to work because stewards bring you coffee and stuff and the very occasional night bird drops by so you don't get bored. I'm working on a new novel and it's going okay so I was very late last night and I stayed in bed late this morning...if only I'd have stayed there all day. I went ashore and took a taxi to the town, I didn't think it worth getting out but I was kinda embarrassed not to, after all the taxi driver lives here. I spun out a stroll around for as long as I could which was ten minutes then took the same taxi back to the ship. Talk about a third world country, it was like a shanty town if only I knew what a shanty town was. And as for hiring a motorbike, I'm not sure even the president has one! I think we only stop here because there is nowhere else to stop, I'm prepared to believe that the capitol, San Jose, is as nice as they say it is but it is also one hundred miles away over rough roads. There is a tour but I'm betting the air conditioning on the coach is broken down and the guide's verbose. There is also a trip to the rain forest I fancied but I was warned off by the two ladies on my table this week, Margaret and Hilda. Apparently it's a nightmarish stumble through a wet swamp and as the locals inform you, the animals only come out at night, so you don't actually see anything. It makes you wonder if any of these backwoods places are worth visiting, it's okay if you're David Attenborough but for normal people who can't afford the shirt it's just too hot and uncomfortable to bother.

    But the best part of the day happened in the evening when I heard about June and John. I avoided them after Columbia and they didn't bother looking for me because we kept being told how peaceful Costa Rica was. Well, they hired a taxi for themselves as there are no limousines or school teacher guides to be had and they went for a day-long drive around the country taking in the rain forest, the nature reserve, San Jose and everything. When it was getting near to 5 they asked the driver to head back as the ship left at 6 and the driver took them to a very dark and deserted part of the forest, stopped the car and declared it broken down. He then proceeded to repair it very slowly and it cost them a $100 tip just to get him to miraculously make the car work again. June and John have gone around telling everybody it wouldn't have happened if they had had SuperNick with them, that the driver wouldn't have dared anything and if he had that I would have soon sorted him out. Bless!

13 Acapulco

It's really slow this week, they say it's the slowest leg of the cruise and that we'll be full again from Los Angeles. Surprisingly it's not as much fun. When it's full you hardly notice the extra people on board because the service is so good but when it's slower lots of stuff gets cancelled. Paula had to cancel the art auction and as she works on commission she was not a happy bunny so we just sat and talked for a while. We are getting a bit close but I'm not going to let it happen, she's a lovely thing but much too young and I'm much too vulnerable still to risk messing up anybody else's life. Still, she's a good mate.

I've finally had to do my washing, you can only wear shirts so often. I was trying to get a lady on my table to do it for me but every time I mentioned it she roared with laughter. I struggled down to the laundrette with a huge load, cor it was like walking into the Nasser Control Centre with all those dials and switches. I stood there pathetically then resolutely approached the nearest machine and thrust the whole lot inside and was immediately rewarded by a positive barrage of eager women who all informed me that I was putting much too much in at once and anyway it was a tumble dryer I had selected. It turned into a kind of laundry seminar come party, I had this lovely Australian lady organising everything for me, she had three machines going at once while I was despatched back to my cabin to fetch hangers for my shirts (apparently you don't have to iron most of them if you put them straight onto hangers. I didn't know this even though I am entirely familiar with the differences between a washing machine and a tumble dryer). An American lady looked after the drying side and in a somewhat intimate manner even mixed some of her laundry in with mine. My dress shirts were taken away by a grumbling Oriental lady (I suppose it could have been the Japanese lady from the dance lesson but our relationship had been so brief it was hard to tell) she would iron away furiously occasionally howling some sort of oriental abuse over her shoulder at me. This is a trait I have become familiar with in women, they will do virtually anything for you if you approach them in the right wáy but will then proceed to tell you off about it. Finally, we were all finished (I use the perpendicular pronoun loosely as I was completely superfluous except as hanger fetcher) so I asked the Australian lady to marry me (I've found out that Big C is empowered to marry us but that the marriage will only legally last for the length of the voyage – ah ha!). She apologised sincerely but said she was already married to a lovely man who would be likely to object. All I could obtain from her was a firm promise that if he was to fall over the side she would keep me in mind.

And so to Acapulco. There was an amazing view of the bay as we steamed in, it was a bit New York–like, but lit by blazing sunshine. The sea is incredible and the curved beach goes on forever. I went ashore about eleven and was immediately fighting my way through a hoard of taxi drivers all shouting at me and waving their fists at each other, I feel a better collective adjective for them would have been a threat of taxi drivers! Anyway, after one particularly annoying driver had tripped over and had sat down with unfortunate vigour they seemed to lose interest and I was free to take a stroll around the town. It was okay, typical sort of tourist place full of jewellers and phone shops and there was a bright blue church that enlivened the whole experience, very Picassoesque. Next I took a quieter taxi ('Si senor, 10 pesetas is worth the same as 6 dollars.') to see the cliff divers. This was very impressive and very well done…and very expensive! These 5 young men took it in turns to leap off this fantastically high cliff to certain death, missing the intervening rocks by seeming inches before plunging spectacularly into the ocean. They then come running up through the crowds collecting money as they go…I found out later that they belong to a closed shop union and make so much money that they retire as virtual millionaires before they are thirty (a bit like the bloody taxi drivers).

    I then took another taxi to the far side of the bay with the intention of walking the 5 miles back. The price of the taxi doubled in the interim and I had a most interesting and psychedelic discussion with the driver where he went through every colour in the visible spectrum and a couple I had never witnessed before. When he had relapsed back to a pinkish—brown normality I gave him the fee we had agreed on at the start which started off the whole thing again. I watched with interest but after a time he seemed to run out of steam and he gave me some sort of blessing (well, I think it was a blessing) before driving off in somewhat of a hurry. It was an okay walk but so hot that I arrived back at the ship absolutely soaking but the only thing of interest was meeting a Mexican who very kindly offered to sell me his sister for $40…I thanked him but told him I already had a sister and that was one too many.

    I was dying for my swim so within 5 minutes I was down in the dark, 4 decks safely away from the sunlight, swimming circuits. It was good, everybody else was ashore so I had the pool to myself but to my annoyance I was only halfway through my mile when this little Japanese man in a suit came in. The suit was somewhat surprising so I stopped to have a look. He dipped a plastic cup in the water then took it to a panel in the wall which he opened with a key. Then he removed some sort of science kit and proceeded to pour the water into 4 test tubes. Next, he added some chemicals to each of the tubes and examined the results, he took it ever so seriously holding the tubes up to the light and studying them intently. As he finished with each tube he heaved a great sigh of relief and put it back in a rack. Then he reached his final sample, took one look at it and jumped like he'd been bayoneted in the bum. 'Ha!' he cried. He then gestured furiously to another be-suited Japanese I hadn't noticed who came hurrying over to examine the sample himself. 'Ha!' he also cried doing the bayonet jump. There was a short, frenzied argument: 'Ah doo…hey tar…mucon ray…shakaa…eeshar …ompare…' and the like, then they hurriedly locked the sample away and rushed away in tandem. It was about this time that I decide to get out of the water. Strangely the pool has been drained ever since and I've developed an itch.

14 Hollywood

I went to a Captain's party last night, you know, the ones I have vowed never to go near again but two ladies on my table told me that this one was for people on the world cruise only and would be completely different. Luckily my clique was there all dressed up except for Dorcus who waited on us dressed in a pinny, I was very complimentary about it until she told me to go away in a very unCunard like manner! We all sat discussing just how bad Big C was at public speaking until Paula realised that his wife was sitting right beside us, oh dear! The two ladies were right, it was completely different, it was much worse. None of the mounds of caviar and vodka lakes I had been promised just the interminable giving away of badges for people who have travelled on the QE2 for 100 days, 500 days, 1000 days and get this, 2000 days…that's six years. Daniella told me that one old lady has been on 17 of the 18 world cruises that the QE2 has undertaken. Apparently, it's the same crowd every year but as one of the menagerie said to me, she can either sit all year in her apartment in

Boston or go around the world and get to go dancing every night. I slipped away early and went to work in the Lido.

There's a very odd man who wanders around at night (no, not me, another odd man) he hasn't got any footsteps, he just materialises at your side like Napoleon was supposed to do. You know, suddenly he's there, it's like having a lizard crawl up your leg. And he always starts talking in the middle of a sentence and in the middle of a conversation like we have been talking for hours. He knows my name and I haven't told him it. Now here's the really sinister bit, no one else has ever seen him, you can describe anyone on the cruise at all and the girls will immediately know who you are talking about, whether they are married, how many kids they have and who they are knocking off, but this bloke no. And I've never seen him in daylight. At least two people die every cruise and I'm wondering if I have happened on the ghost of one of them, could be, though he's certainly sound on English politics and I'm not totally convinced a ghost would bother, I mean how would it effect him? Anyway, after a short, but vigorous political debate, he suddenly trolls off and he goes away up the passageway without bending his knees like he has wheels under his soles. Ah well, I must remember to buy some garlic in L.A.

Hurray for Hollywood! I took the tour: Hollywood, Los Angeles, Beverley Hills. L.A. was pretty good, much cleaner than you'd think from the movies and everything was very big and spread out with wide streets. Trouble was that everyone else on the coach was foreign and do you know that most of them couldn't speak English? Even when I shouted it at them! Now, I don't want to be intolerant, and I certainly don't believe in going to extremes, but I do think it should be an iron rule that anyone who can't speak English by the age of ten should be thrown into prison until they can, it's easy enough, I learned it when I was two!

Hollywood is like a tacky Brentwood (yes, yes, an even tackier Brentwood). There are beggars everywhere in the streets, brightly dressed ladies who seem to be trying to sell something but I never did find out quite what, cheap gift shops and not a hint of glamour anywhere. I went to the Chinese theatre to see the footprints and even this had a booth up offering: ***Your own footprints in concrete $25.*** I've said it before, you never should visit these places, you read all about them and get a glamorised view then in a few short minutes it gets smashed for life. I went on the footprints walk but a big black man was being sick over Dorothy Lamour and it ruined it for me.

Beverley Hills was better but there wasn't a pretzel in sight. It's a bit like Bond Street with hideous clothes at hideous prices and hideous jewellery with no prices. There were no stars anywhere of course, and I don't blame them, they probably can't afford to shop there. I was walking innocently down Rodeo Drive (how's that for name dropping?) when four great black men came swaggering along and eased me into the street. I told the one that if it was true he had purchased the street then he should inform me and I would then stand politely aside. I further ventured the opinion that if any of them ever visited England then I hoped they would be treated with more courtesy than they had shown me. The leading black man, who was wearing some kind of uniform, came back and apologised most charmingly and eloquently considering he was handicapped by the fact that someone at some time had removed most of his front teeth. I've said it before, all the races are the same (except for Germans of course) they always respond well to the polite approach even when it is shouted at them.

I went a bit further and found the Hollywood budget-rent-a-car only on display there were: two Ferraris, two Mercedes, any number of Rolls Royces and BMWs, and an assorted mix of sports cars that included an AC Cobra, a Lamborghini, a Jaguar XJS and a Morgan plus 8. The jewellers too have to be seen to be believed. I went into one and after a brief glance in my direction all three of the staff wrote me off as a potential customer and went back to their discussion on American football. I wandered around, it makes you wonder how women can walk around wearing such massive chunks of rock, they must feel like SCUBA divers. I thanked the three serving staff for their courteous and fulsome service and returned to the coach, rockless.

There was another crowd on the sidewalk (pavement) with more Japanese tourists taking pictures of nothing, Germans arguing volubly with their guide, French people sneering at everybody, English still waiting to be introduced, and I pushed my way unceremoniously through them and up the steps of the coach. 'It's a snare and delusion,' said I to the sitting multitude, 'I don't believe any film stars live here.'

Everybody gave me a cheer and this I agreed with but misunderstood the reason why they had only just started doing it. The guide then told me that if I had looked a little more closely when falling out with the four black men I would have noticed that they were surrounding Elton John who stood quietly while his chief bodyguard apologised to me. Furthermore, the crowd of anxious tourists I had pushed through were all trying to take photographs of John Travolta…my cohorts on the coach had been much impressed by the way I had ignored him with such aplomb.

15 Hawaii

We've got three days at sea now before Honolulu and I'm relieved but it does make you wonder if I'm becoming institutionalised not wanting to go ashore. I rarely even go up on deck, I can't see the point, I don't sunbathe, it's always either too hot or windy and there are much better seats inside. However, I fancied a short stroll this morning and I was right, it was both too hot and windy but following the ship was a school of dolphin (I think it should be dolphins) and I watched it for ages. It's turned quite rough, I'm thinking of suing Cunard, they promised me sunshine and calm seas and this morning when I woke up all the pictures were on the floor and my bedside table had spilled its contents all over me, all without waking me up. It's a bit odd, this sleeping at sea, I went back to my cabin last night to change out of my dinner jacket, it was about twelve, I sat on the bed for a minute and woke up at eleven the following morning and we'd gained an hour as well. Oh, I was cross, a whole night's work gone so I did a couple of hours in the morning instead. I was working away in the Grand Lounge, Paula was also there doing something with her pictures and all is quiet and peaceful. I have developed a habit of working with one leg up on the desk, it kinda relieves the stress on my back but as I wear shorts it prompts people to make remarks about my legs, funny at first but after a very short time this starts to pall. A little bearded man hovered into the edge of my vision, 'Nice leg,' says he. Me, 'My, aren't we original?' There is a brief silence, then, 'Is this a good place to work?' obviously he is still there. Me, 'No, rude people keep on interrupting me.' This works and he disappears: Hurrah! Paula, 'Nick you did know that was the Captain you were speaking to didn't you?' 'Of course,' I nodded sagely, 'I never think it's wise to get too familiar with the driver, do you?' Oh shit! Perhaps I'd better give the next few Captain's parties a miss.

Incidentally, Paula introduced me to this very old wizened woman at the last party, I couldn't work out why.

Then she told me she had successfully sued Cunard and had been awarded two free world cruises. Why? Well, she slipped on some spilled liquid and damaged her leg and she claimed it meant she couldn't have sex for the rest of the cruise.

I'm still falling out with Germans. I didn't realise what a bunch they are: they stride arrogantly right up to you in the passageways expecting you to get out of their way (they are invariably disappointed in this), they push in front of you in lifts and they stand in doorways having long conversations, this last they do even if they see you waiting…but not twice. Then, get this, I went for my normal swim yesterday afternoon trusting that the be-suited Japanese water tester had got it put right. I had been trolling up and down the empty pool for about thirty odd lengths when this great fat cow comes oozing down the steps. She summons me with an imperious hand and proceeds to inform me that she has a bad leg and would require the sole use of the shallow end of the pool in case I knocked into it. Furthermore she tells me that I must be sure not to splash as it disturbs her. I told her that I wasn't Poland and if she intended to invade my territory then she'd end up like the Bismarck (there were similarities). She stormed majestically away to complain to Iona but Iona is a friend and so she got short shrift, ha ha!

When we were ashore in Costa Rica there was a very tiny earthquake, so tiny I didn't even mention it in this journal. Well, I've just learned that one daft woman had to be helped back to the ship suffering from shock and she has been in the hospital ever since. This brings to mind the barmy woman in the cabin opposite mine who spends her whole life standing in the doorway, clutching the doorjamb, crying. Any offers of help are met by a sudden increase in the intensity of her distress and the protestation: 'Leave me, I'm just being silly.' You sort of get used to it, like a haemorrhoid, anybody new on board always gets sucked in to trying to help her but soon gets fed up and joins the rest of us in apathy. Yesterday afternoon I asked her if she could cry a bit more quietly as I was trying to sleep, I can't work out whether or not she is German.

    We berthed in Hawaii at about ten o clock in the morning and I got off about eleven. Honolulu is a bit like New York only the traffic is heavier. I went for a stroll and found a bank because one of the problems I have is that I haven't any money. I'm not at all sure what I have in the bank, the Poison Dwarf did all that sort of stuff, and how I've managed to live up to now is beyond me but it was well time to get hold of some money. The bank wouldn't accept my driver's licence as proof of identity but amazingly advanced me $500 on the strength of my SCUBA card. They also took my fingerprints, there's a little ink pad on the counter and you have to leave a thumbprint on the back of every transaction. I was half expecting a finger up the bottom job but obviously they aren't yet as sophisticated as the New York Police department as all I got was a friendly smile. They did let me make a free phone call to book a motorbike but when I arrived at the dealers they refused to rent me this huge Harley because my license didn't cover it. I ran into this problem in the Caribbean but there they have this very sensible rule that you either need a full motorcycle license or a $20 bill. This doesn't apply in Hawaii so after having a bit of a rant at the dealer I stormed off down the road still shouting, all most enjoyable: I'd hurl some abuse back over my shoulder and he'd bawl some back at me. I think we were both a bit sad when I was finally out of earshot.

There was a tatty little rental agency, well agency is the wrong word, mud hut would be closer, just up the road and a tatty little old man rented me this tatty little old scooter. I mean, we are talking pre-war here! It was seriously held together with duct tape and bits of wire but funnily enough I kinda liked it and it was the old man's sole asset and he was absolutely thrilled to get the business. So off I went, roaring like a tractor, smoke billowing all around me, and entered into the solid mass of BMWs and Mercedes. The great thing about this scooter it was so old it was as loose as a Frenchwoman on VE night and it went like a bomb (a bit like the Frenchwomen, or so my Dad said). I beat this beautiful new motorbike away from the traffic lights and you should have seen his face, he looked like he'd just experienced the New York police department's initiation ceremony. I went upwards, heading around the island and keeping to the coast so I had a chance of finding my way home and the beaches are incredible, the best I have ever seen, it nearly made me want to sunbathe…but not quite!

I was about ten miles out when the brakes failed and this made driving even more hazardous than normal for me. I'd already had a spell of wondering why the traffic coming towards me was on the wrong side of the road and moreover was all flashing its lights, still I couldn't take it back because I had no idea where the tatty old man's business was. I stopped in Waikiki by running into a tree and had three waffle cones from Baskin Robins for lunch. This cheered me up enormously then I had a jumbo hot dog for pudding which depressed me again. They just can't do hot dogs anywhere but Britain, what's the good of onions unless they are fried? I fed mine to the ducks who were casually strolling down the street, as far as I can work out they were at least three miles from the nearest water. Then after another hour or so of struggling with the traffic and the brakes I managed to find my way back to the ship, impressed eh? Well, I did have a bit of help, I was steaming past thinking I was miles from home when it gave one of its hoots. I like to think it was Big C calling me home but I will also countenance the idea that he was merely clearing out his pipes.

If only I had left it there! But it was only five and still light so I decided to visit Pearl Harbour. Now, on Hawaii, there are these massive motorways but the problem is that you aren't allowed to take motor scooters on them but I couldn't find another way so I thought sod it, I'm British, I can go anywhere. So, I'm roaring along at an absolute top speed of 60 and all the other traffic is doing more than 180 when my motorway merges with another. Cor! Talk about hairy, I'm in the middle of six lanes of traffic still doing 60 while everybody is shaking their fists and blowing their horns at me. Well, no, that's not strictly accurate because one of them isn't blowing his horn he is sounding his siren. I've been Hawaii fiveoed!

There's the standard great fat American cop and a jolly little Hawaiian and they both come swaggering towards me. I get off my scooter and stop the engine though that's not difficult because the engine fails whenever I misguidedly let the revs drop to less than a howl. I take off my helmet, another less than difficult task because it is at least five sizes too big for me and has only half of one strap. 'Hello,' I greet them happily. The fat cop speaks, 'Don't you know you aren't allowed to take motor scooters on the main highway?' he demands. 'Yes,' says I not seeing the point of lying. 'Well, what do you imagine you are doing then?' he asks nonplussed. 'I imagine I am breaking the law,' says Honest Nick. This seems to amuse the jolly little cop who starts chuckling, it amuses the other one not at all. Meanwhile the vertically challenged cop is strolling around my scooter studying it in a bemused fashion. 'This is getting on a bit,' he says and unwisely gives it a kick. The starting pedal immediately drops off with a clatter. 'Damn,' he says, 'who did you hire this from, the Flintstones?' Now, this made me laugh, it still does, but you should have seen the effect it had on the cop who starts to howl with mirth at his own wit. The horizontally gifted cop is still unmoved, 'Well, you sure as hell can't ride it any further,' he says. The other one pipes up, 'Well, what do you want him to do with it Arnie?' asks the Benny Hill of the Hawaiian police, 'wait until it rusts away?' More gales of laughter from two of the assembled company.

  The upshot was I was given a police escort to the next exit which happened to be for the airport. I waved gaily at them but only the happy one waved back. I must have driven around that bloody airport ten times and I still couldn't find another road home. Well, it was getting dark, and I was getting lonely, and I hadn't eaten since Baskin Robins, and I thought they'd be gone by this time, so…I was bombing along the highway at 60 miles an hour while everybody else was doing at least 180 when guess who I met coming the other way? Swipe me but one of them was cross, I'll leave you to guess which one. But he was cross, more than cross, furious, enraged, no, none of these words really portray the intensity of his emotions. Murderous, that's the one! He was murderous. I think it was a toss up whether to book me or shoot me dead.

  Finally, they had me sitting in the car, which to be brutally frank wasn't a lot posher than my scooter (but I thought it unpolitic to mention it at the time) while they radioed Steve McGarret back at headquarters. I've been officially cautioned, informed that if I commit another offence on Hawaiian soil in the next year then it will be vigorously pursued and made to promise to return the scooter first thing in the morning…shame: book him Dano!

Otherwise it was an ordinary kind of day.

Have you ever noticed how things look completely the opposite the following day? Somehow the dramas with the cops seemed less important, their warnings less ominous. The thing was that I still hadn't seen Pearl Harbour, and the taxi fare was $15 each way, and I was still in possession of a perfectly good scooter…well, it ran anyway, even if it didn't stop too well. The previous night I left it leaning against a bollard in the tow-away zone so I didn't expect it to be there but it was in all it's emaciated glory. I felt a warm glow of affection when I saw it standing there waiting for me right next to this fat Australian who was bemoaning the fact that his car had been taken to the pound – ha, ha. I sat astride it (the scooter not the fat Australian) thinking: I was supposed to be taking it right back to the rental place but surely no one could object if I dropped in at Pearl Harbour on the way. To be absolutely accurate it wasn't quite on the way because it lay in exactly the opposite direction but if you apply Richmal Crompton's **William's** definition: it was on the way there in the sense you could get there from it! I was equipped with directions this time because I had learned, from Big C's wife no less (she's Hawaiian) that the alternative route to the main highway is called Niemitz

Highway, they don't say it's an alternative route or anything obvious like that you're just expected to know.

    Pearl Harbour is very interesting, certainly the most interesting thing on Hawaii, inanimate that is. I'm still carrying on with my survey of women's breasts but the female population of Hawaii is from so many different cultures it is hardly relevant. I went to see everything: the museum, the battleship, the submarine, the one thing I didn't visit was the sea memorial to the ***Arizona,*** because it's only a bit of concrete and you can't get near it for Japanese taking photographs. The museum was better than most other museums, I tried getting around it for cheap like I did the MOMA, by using my student's card but the huge American GI plug ugly on the door was unimpressed and I didn't feel like pushing it. You could go everywhere on the ships, the only annoying thing was the patronising manner in which the guide urged you to keep your head down on entering the submarine, they always sound like they are talking to children, I brushed away his protestations somewhat bruskly. Talk about claustrophobia, you simply cannot imagine spending months under the sea in that thing. I retired to the battleship, more my idea of fun, at least you've got a chance if the damn thing goes down. The tour around the battleship was good but I had trouble appreciating it because I was still recovering from the stunning blow on the head I had received when I suddenly stood upright in the sleeping berths of the submarine.

    Next on the agenda was to take the scooter back and in this I was somewhat handicapped because I had absolutely no idea where the rental place was and the tatty old man hadn't furnished me with any paperwork. I decided to revert to my normal methods, that is to drive around randomly hoping to spot the old man's shop…the fact that this method has never worked for me in the past has still not deterred me from pursuing it on all possible occasions and may well give some explanation as to my prevalence for getting lost. But, ah ha, for the first time in my life it worked: I was booming along a duel carriageway when I noticed a Harley Davison on the other side of the road sitting on the pavement so, on the off chance, I humped the scooter over the crash barrier and to my amazement found it was the original place where I had tried to hire a motorbike. Even I could find the old man from there and within five minutes I was in his shop only now it was being manned (is that the correct word?) by a woman. She turned out to be the old man's daughter and she was vastly relieved to see me back alive. She had popped out to get them some lunch the previous day leaving strict instructions to her father not to rent anything out because all their bikes had been prebooked by the sailors from an American warship. The old man, who is half senile (I didn't notice anything, he looked okay to me), had rented me his own scooter which he only uses to travel about a hundred yards a day to work. The woman, who was surprisingly from Hastings, was so apologetic that she didn't want to charge me but I couldn't stand the thought of the disappointment in the old man's eyes and we worked out a deal.

    All in all I think we can write Hawaii up as a success.

16 Pago Pago

I've got a new dance partner, her name's Ardy. Obviously she is American and at 60 odd she is quite young for this ship. She's good fun to dance with and very forgiving, unlike some of the other women who are odd to say the least. One I admire, dances with her walking frame as her partner, she's better than everyone else! Another is the fattest woman I have ever seen, she would make Dawn French look sylphlike, and if you pair up with her your arms won't make it around her impressive girth so she keeps sliding away from you, it's rather like trying to hold onto a greasy barrage balloon. Then there's a Japanese lady who walks around the dance floor grumbling to herself, it's like she's not part of the dance class because she never actually does any of the dancing, just grumbles about it. There's another Japanese lady who only wants to dance with herself, if you offer to partner up with her she shouts at the top of her voice: 'No! No, partners!' She's a real trip that one. And this other couple, they listen to Warren (the dance instructor) intently and are the ones who always ask him questions, then when the music starts they just stand there swaying to it. No, Ardy and me are quite normal compared to the others.

Another enormously fat woman never steps on the dance floor, or in fact never seems to step anywhere if she can help it. She isn't as fat as the other woman but her fatness has none of the jolly, riotous nature of the barrage balloon who goes cannoning off the other dancers all the time roaring with laughter. No, this one's fatness is a kind of slothful fatness, it's loose and keeps on moving after she's stopped, like she's got a stomach full of ferrets. The other thing that makes her an interesting subject to observe is that she sleeps all the time, and I do mean: ***all the time!*** She goes to concerts and snores through them, she nearly drowned out the piano player the other night. She attends lectures, goes to the cinema, sits in exhibitions, and sleeps through them all. I even caught her sleeping in the front row of the disco last night, apparently she even goes on the ludicrously expensive outside trips and stays on the coach to sleep. As I write she is sitting in a chair at the other end of the corridor snoring away. When I come down (or up) in the morning she'll still be there her fat sort of pushed up around her and hanging over the edge of the chair like some obscene kind of winding cloth. I wondered if she was dead the first evening and nobody had noticed so I gave her a investigatory prod: after an age she sort of struggled up out of her sea of fat and grunted at me, it was remarkably like watching a hippopotamus getting out of a mud bath. Apparently, I was lucky. John woke her one night in the cinema and she went berserk, accusing him of sexually assaulting her. John, who isn't fussy, said it wasn't the sexual assault charge that worried him but the idea of anybody thinking he would sexually assault her.

So, to Pago Pago. It's really pronounced Pango Pango or by the locals, Pongo Pongo. It's actually American Samoa which is good because I only ever have American dollars. I've learned the fiddle, you can cash a cheque in the casino and get the best rate of exchange in the world but they only deal in dollars…and I thought it was a British ship.

I liked Pago Pago. I disembarked about 10 o clock and brother, was it hot! Not as hot as Egypt but certainly the hottest place yet on this trip. Half of the people got straight back on board and hid behind the air conditioning units. I can't understand these people, they book a South Sea cruise then moan because it's hot. They are the same ones who got on board at New York and then when we left harbour they all started complaining: **'Oh, the ship's moving!'** Tell me, what did they expect it to do?

There were no motorbikes so I hired a car from the local hotel and it was a beauty, I've no idea what it was but it was big and shiny and went like a bomb. So, off I trolled around the island, the sea and the beaches are incredible and the interior one huge mountainous rain forest, greenery at last…you don't realise how much you miss it! I plunged into the mountains and blimey, they've no sense of proportion these Pago Pagoans, where we would put a cable car, they put a road. I was inching down this sheer drop thinking I needed some pitons and an abseil rope when my brakes failed. The wonderful thing was I wasn't even surprised, as my car took off like a dragster driven by the local champion I sat there placidly thinking: 'Oh yes, my brakes have failed again.' It has a certain sort of natural order…Nick hires a vehicle…the brakes fail! After I had taken a couple of hairpin bends at close on Mach 2 I managed to get the automatic gear lever into *low* so I went through the village at the base of the mountain at only 70mph, which isn't bad considering there is a 30mph speed limit governing the whole island. I stopped because I felt disinclined to carry on driving at that precise moment and decided to have a little walk instead. I staggered out of the car and let forth a couple of screams, I don't really know why, I just kinda felt like doing it at the time. Then I noticed that smoke was pouring from the back wheels and, thinking that this was less than normal, even for an American car, I stopped to check. And, yes, the brakes had failed because I had left the handbrake on. I haven't done that since school! Still, if I had to do it then I guess it was somewhat inevitable that I would do it on mountainous Pago Pago.

    I thought I'd better give the brakes time to cool off a bit so I strolled back to the village. It was virtually deserted but then I found everyone gathered together at the local coffee shop. It looked a bit like an open air bus shelter but being no snob (and terribly thirsty) I joined them for coffee. Everybody was lovely, so friendly and welcoming and when I was served coffee all mention of paying was waved away in a sunburst of smiling faces. Everybody then turned their chairs to face the front where a funny little man with a bandage around his head was standing. Ah, thought Nick, entertainment! It was too, he starts by howling abuse at us but the good bit was that he kept pausing and we would all howl back. I was encouraged to join in and did so enthusiastically, it didn't matter what we actually howled, it was the volume that mattered. It was gradually dawning on me that this was a pretty rum sort of café and the somewhat frequent times when we all knelt down we weren't thanking the man for his coffee, but that today was Sunday and this was a church. I had wondered why, when I was driving around the island, that most places seemed to be closed. I wandered back to the car after running the gauntlet of the entire villager's farewells to find that my brakes were working again.

I drove back to the ship and went to see my little waitress, Noor, who had put together a picnic for me bless her. Then I went and met Paula and Daniella. I found them on a beach they had told me about earlier and was welcomed warmly and my picnic even more so. We sat around eating it, which I found difficult because when Daniella sat up she was topless again and…well, I mean, where are you supposed to look? Then Paula and I went snorkelling, amazing, after British childhood holidays you just can't believe the sea can be that warm, no, not warm, hot! You hear people talk about sea as hot as bathwater and you think: oh yes, right, but you literally have to come out to cool off. The fish were amazing, it was almost as good as SCUBA diving, even my favourite little blue fish were there. There was this tiny hole in the coral so I stuck my finger in it and it's infuriated inhabitant came raging out and bit me. You can rather see its point, I imagine I'd be less than happy if I was in my living room and someone stuck his great fat finger though the window. Trouble was it was right at the limit of my dive so I couldn't get at the little bastard to give it a smack. I got back to the ship late to have a shower only to find I was sunburnt (Heaven only knows how Daniella fared) and furthermore my finger had all swollen up. I am now left wondering what it was that bit me, if it was a sea snake then this journal will end right here.

17 Fiji

There's a particularly unusual woman on board. She's very short and very American and she styles herself as the Diva of the QE2. She even has a T-shirt with it emblazoned on the front and she always signs herself as the QE2 Diva. She spends her entire day going around serenading people. If you are sitting quietly having a drink in the pub she will suddenly appear opposite you, take your hand softly in hers, and break into song. She stopped doing this to me when I enthusiastically joined in with ***O Sole Mio*** and my voice completely drowned hers out. And, of course, as it's the QE2, she truly has the most dreadful voice, it's a cross between a live pig being slowly roasted over hot coals and a weasel having its testicles nailed to the floor. She, though, thinks she is wonderful! We have a classical performer on once a week and this week it was a famous opera singer, well, they tell me he's famous as I've never heard of him but then again he probably has never heard of me either. Anyway, our Diva trapped him in the bar afterwards to compare notes and she managed to give him a few pointers on his performance. When we went to Hollywood we visited the Hollywood Bowl, you know where the Beatles performed? Well, it was surprisingly tatty, and the seats! They were real bum botherers. Everybody was standing in a group listening to the guide except for me who had done my wandering off thing. Our Diva climbs up onto the stage and starts to sing. The hilarious thing was that everybody was listening intently to the guide but the second our Diva hit her first note (or failed to hit it) every single member of the party turned in unison, like a brigade of Life Guards on parade, and rushed for the exit. Apparently, it all happened so quickly that the guide was left still talking and she gradually ran down when she finally caught on that her entire audience had disappeared.

And the thing is, she gets a free cruise! I checked and it's true. Apparently she has forged such a place for herself that Cunard now gives her a free world cruise every year. I couldn't believe that Cunard was so hard up for entertainment…and then I was offered a job. I've been dating this girl from the library and she phoned her boss in Banbury who arranges the various acts, lecturers, pianists, theatre groups etc who entertain us. What they want is for me to give a series of lectures on writing on the next world cruise. The deal is that I get a top cabin and I eat in the Queens Restaurant (the posh one, it's ghastly, everybody is very quiet and well behaved) all I have to do is give three forty-five minute lectures a week. Well, we'll see but you aren't really getting anywhere are you?

    This girl from the library, Carol, I started dating her a week or so ago. I was getting too close to Paula so I started seeing Carol as a kind of anaesthetic. The thing is, she's a bit wet and not that attractive, she's very hairy, in fact she has a sort of small moustache. We dance together every night and we are great at this, when you've danced the Tango with hairy Carol you don't need sex, you just skip right to the post activity cigarette.

    Fiji? I didn't like Fiji. I didn't like the people. I felt at any time I might get stuffed into an earth oven and used to supplement their rather meagre diet. I know that they are descended from a much fiercer people than other South Sea Islanders, and Carol assures me that under a hundred years ago they were practising cannibalism as a norm, so perhaps my outlook is a bit jaded, but I didn't like them at all. I hired a car and had to fill in scads of forms all making me promise not to take the car into the interior, not to stop in remote villages and never, ever to pick anybody up. You can imagine how I felt as I set off. It must have been a bit like when the British Government dispatched food officer Warren Maine to advise on the famine that was sweeping

Belgium in the 18th century. Still he managed to help with the food crisis…they ate him!

I thought the main town would be fairly safe so I stopped by a long row of cars and did a very impressive bit of reverse parking in a space smaller than my car. A gang of youths watched me cynically then gave me a spontaneous round of applause when I was successful. I bowed to them then marched arrogantly off doing my little Englander act. What a dump! There was abso-bloody-lutely nothing to see, I wouldn't have ventured into any of the coffee bars unless I was wearing a biohazard suit. I walked the length of the town and all I found was a tacky hardware shop that sold me some picture hooks. Thinking that I now had my excuse for stopping, I mean, you can't go telling the inhabitants of a town that the whole place stinks can you, I made my way back to the car. And then the horrible truth hit me: I had just got into the car when I hired it and had been concentrating on the gang of youths when I parked so I had no idea what it looked like. No really, not an inkling, not the colour, the make and I sure as hell hadn't left anything inside it that would be familiar. After a few seconds of intense thought I came up with a solution so, taking a deep breath, I went to one end and started off down the long row of cars trying my key. The best bit was these four old men sitting on a pavement bench smoking those old-fashioned curly pipes. They didn't say a word, just followed me with their eyes, the further I went the more smoke they puffed out and by the time I located my car they were almost totally obscured in a kind of pea-souper. I turned and gave them a triumphant wave and they all gave me a solemn nod back, they must have thought I was an incredibly bad car thief.

I drove around a bit more but the whole place is dry and barren and all the houses are shacks roofed with corrugated iron. I crept back to the ship for lunch, I had been ashore for less than two hours. I went to my cabin to find that Lito had left a note on my pillow. It was from the Captain inviting me to dine on his table for the following week. Now, I don't know whether it's just me, but all this fuss made of the Captain gets up my nose, after all, he's just the driver. They expect you to stand in a queue for half an hour just to shake his hand and, as I have previously related, only to have it grabbed so you are catapulted past him so you don't waste his time talking. The whole crew now know that I find this highly offensive because I went to a meeting about the Taj Mahal visit and this little turd, 23rd officer cadet or something, tried to do the same only I was stronger than him and he ended up halfway across the room, upside down in a pile of chairs. I also have trouble respecting anybody who spends their whole life at sea so I was less than impressed by the invite. Not that it was special, apparently they try and seat everybody on the world cruise at his table at least once…and they have to wait! When the Captain's late, and he is always late, the waiters won't come near the table in case you do the unheard of and start without him. I should coco! So I drafted a little note back declining the offer as I was perfectly happy with my companions on ***my*** table. Then I added a naughty little footnote, I suggested that if the Captain wanted to meet me socially then we had a free seat at ***my*** table after New Zealand. Somehow this got around the ship and it is the first time any passenger has ever turned the Captain down that anybody can remember…fame at last!

We had a meeting of my group last night: Paula, Dorcus and Daniella. They have decided that I am as normal as I am ever going to be, I haven't hit anybody, or shouted, or monopolised someone for hours while I related my sad story to them…none of which I admitted to doing but the girls insisted. So we went up to the boat deck with all my tablets: the Valium and the Prozac, even the Panadol. I explained how it was vital to come off the Prozac slowly and we gazed at the packet reflectively for a moment then chucked the lot over the side and went off to get sloshed to celebrate…I feel better than I have for months.

18 New Zealand

It's finally been confirmed: I'm a thundering idiot. I've always suspected I was but now it's official, the custom inspector in Auckland told me so! In fact he told everybody in a radius of five miles that I was a thundering idiot. More of that later.

One of the main problems I encounter with the QE2 is the constant announcements, one is going on while I type this. It's bad enough listening to them once but they are then repeated in French, German, and once to my horror, in Japanese. They take no account of the fact that I sleep in the afternoon but I've fixed that since I got at the speaker in my room with my trusty Swiss army penknife. The announcements are particularly bad on arrival in port, there's a positive barrage of information of things you cannot take into the country: Armalite assault rifles, atomic bombs, heroin or enraged gorillas…things you really need to know. These are enforced by a booklet that arrives under your door every morning.

  We arrived in New Zealand for an overnight stay. This is a waste of time because you can see everything New Zealand has to offer in one day but I rather think it's so all the crew get a chance to go ashore. Lito woke me about ten with my breakfast as is normal, I can't face the dining hall that early. I got ready and because I was hoping to get one or two things I took my small rucksack and I put in some fruit for lunch, as I'm not too keen on eating much ashore (except for pretzels). So, all in all it had gone eleven when I wandered ashore. There are banners everywhere giving us yet more information on custom controls and a thing called the Amnesty Bin where you can dump anything illegal free of consequences. You can put ten pounds of heroin in there if you like and you're safe from prosecution. I'm not too sure of your chances of getting an enraged gorilla in there though. There were two big jovial custom officers waving us through as QE2 passengers don't get searched. I swung my rucksack off my back to get through the gates and the top came open and an apple and two bananas landed right at the custom officer's feet. He glanced downwards and all vestiges of joviality drained away. He turned a gaze on me that reminded me of my old headmaster just before he used the phrase: 'This is going to hurt me more than it hurts you Walker!' (I always used to think…give yourself a break then). The Headmaster look alike finally found his voice and he rattled off a series of questions like the Star Trek computer: Didn't I know that it was illegal to bring fruit into New Zealand? Was I not aware that New Zealand was the last country in the Southern Hemisphere not to have the apple tree blight? Did I really want to be the person responsible for wiping out New Zealand's fruit harvest? Had not Cunard informed me of this? Had I not received a government printed brochure explaining this to me? Had I not just walked under a banner reminding me of the seriousness of bringing fruit into the country? Had I not noticed the Amnesty bin with its list of undesirable items displayed on the front in five languages? Was I a communist agent intent on wrecking New Zealand's balance of payments? Did I not realise that I could receive up to five years in jail for contravening the regulations? When I was quite sure he had finished I was able to give a totally truthful answer: no, no, no, probably, yes, yes, yes, no, no.

This is the point where he informed me, in a voice I still consider louder than necessary, that I was a thundering idiot. Again I was able to supply a truthful opinion: absolutely! A body search followed when I had everything, including parts of me I don't even allow my doctor to handle, patted most thoroughly. They confiscated my apple and bananas and bundled me off into the city of Auckland. The loud customs officer seemed to have lost interest in me by this time and to be more concerned about a lost dog because he kept on muttering to himself something about not being let off the leash.

Auckland is huge! Bigger than London, I bet you didn't know that, anyway I don't expect it's true. I thought it would be a cute seaside town about the size of Penzance. I wandered vaguely around and the prices are brilliant. I bought 8 CDs for under ten pounds the lot. I had a young lady cut my hair and believed I had struck lucky because when she had finished she gave me a head and upper body massage. Nothing transpired after this and it was later, back on the ship, that Dorcus told me this was quite usual for New Zealand. Next I went up the City Tower which is supposed to be higher than the Eiffel Tower and it's from here you really see how big Auckland is. The people are friendly and helpful, such a change after the surly Europeans I meet on board. But I had to cut the trip short because I no longer had any lunch and I was going out on the evening to the world cruise party.

The world cruise party is the biggest event of the cruise and it is held ashore. The only people invited are those who have already completed a world cruise and there are over 600 of those on board, but they invited me anyway, I'm not sure why after my run ins with Big C. I nearly didn't go because none of my companions was on the guest list but in the end I toddled off. It was held in a show-jumping ring, the one you see on television, and you had to walk between rows of the most beautiful horses to get to the dining area. There was an outside ring set up where a friendly competition was being held but the difference was that the horses were some of the finest in the world. The dinner was very a la carte, so a la carte I couldn't even tell what I was eating, but the service was so terrible that it wasn't really worth eating when you finally got it. But there was so much free drink available that it hardly mattered, right from champagne when you went in, through red and white wines right through to sweet Sauternes with the desert so all the British went back half cut. There was dancing and entertainment on all night long and then towards the end this Maori troop came on and performed the Hukka. They then invited people onto the stage to join them and once again karate came in useful for the Hukka is done in horse riding stance…for the rest of my life I can say I've done the Hukka with the Maoris! I think I may have had a little too much to drink because at the end of the dance I tapped one of the Maoris on the shoulder and asked to borrow his pole, which is a six foot length of thick wood. Now, the only karate weapon I ever teach is the bo which is almost the exact size and shape of the Maori pole so I treated everybody to an impromptu performance, I was great (and very lucky because I didn't drop it) whirling the bow above my head and spinning it around my body. It's easy to impress when you are the guest but the Maoris all cheered me and the passengers went wild, I even saw Big C giving me a bit of a clap. A definite success there.

    The most important thing with a party is to leave on a high so when my little black friend, Arleta (the one I argue with on my table) collapsed after consuming two bottles of wine I half carried her to the coach and took her back to the ship…and they said I needed Prozac.

19 Sydney

And so to Australia. To be honest I've never hankered after visiting Australia, I simply didn't fancy it somehow but apparently it is the most popular section of the cruise. I thought it was all loud Australians telling anti-Brit jokes and heat and flies and drunken Aussies…but it's not! All the Australians I met were very friendly and they seem to have a cheerful affection for the British. They're not like us, of course, the best way I can describe it is it is as if Bob Hoskins had wandered into a Royal Garden Party. But they have a quaint attitude to signs that I absolutely adore. Basically, there aren't any…well, very few. It took me an hour to find the monorail and then the ride only lasted fifteen minutes, and I've taken a photograph of the two signs in the precinct at the bottom of the EMB tower. I don't know what EMB stands for but it is yet another huge building that declares it is the highest in the Southern Hemisphere, or Western Hemisphere, or something. Anyway, these two signs are on the same pole, they both read toilets and they point in exactly opposite directions. This fascinated me so I went in search of someone who could explain and when this bloke did explain that was when I decided that I liked Australians. 'We haven't got any toilets mate,' said he through a mouthful of gum. I pointed to the two signs, 'Ah,' he said, 'you see we're supposed to be getting some…but we haven't decided yet where we are going to put them.' Wonderful! When you do find toilets the signs on them are great too, they are exactly the same for both men and women. I mean: **exactly the same**! I, of course, went in the wrong one and met a very nice lady who agreed that indeed the signs were the same but if you looked hard enough the jacket on the one could be viewed as a dress and visa versa and she found nothing wrong in this explanation. She was a very nice lady though and I nearly asked her to show me around Sydney but you never know where these things might end and if the relationship resulted in marriage then imagine having to tell everybody where we met. On the same theme, my very favourite signs are the pedestrian crossing lights, these stay at red forever so everybody just ignores them. This is, I feel, a most splendid idea because the Germans of course obey them totally so what you get at every intersection is people peacefully crossing the road and a wedge of Germans who have been there since before dawn.

Sydney was good. I could live there if it wasn't for this feeling you get that you are so far away from world affairs. It's clean and open and happy. The harbour is wonderful, and everything happens there at night, it's a bit like St Ives with ice cream sellers and popcorn and hot dogs (with fried onions) and street performers and artists…when you think about it it's not a bit like St Ives.

We were there for two days and on the first night I had booked the Sydney Opera House visit. Now, sour-faced cynic though I may be, I have always wanted to visit this amazing building and so, not wanting to find it fully booked, I had paid some $200 over to Cunard. This was for a coach there and back, a glass of champagne, a ticket to see an opera and a guided tour. Well, we could have walked the 100 yards because we were literally moored just up from it and the coach had to drop us miles away so we probably had to walk further. An aside, rumour has it that the architect was so wrapped up in his genius design that he forgot about car parks and this was only spotted on opening night when all the celebs were left dashing miles through pouring rain.

    We got to the opera house to find that our guide had eloped with one of the sous chefs and neither of them were heard of again and there was no guided tour, so it wasn't all bad. We never did find the glass of champagne and the tickets were very available and very cheap. Still, I'm a fan of both the QE2 and Cunard so I'll not say anymore. The building is truly fantastic but surprisingly the inside is quite sparse and the seats are a horrible cheap plastic, like those in shopping malls that are deliberately designed to limit your sitting in them to under twenty minutes. I sat down in my nasty little seat to watch a rather odd arrangement of three mini operas but fate was about to play another trick on me, this no longer surprises me, I've been singled out all my life for these little incidents. There are on the cruise two enormously fat men. We are talking elephant here. I have no sympathy, how anyone can let themselves get into that condition is beyond me…and if you are that big surely you have to accept that there are certain things you can't do: like fly cheaply or visit the Whispering Gallery at St Pauls…or go to operas in cheap plastic seats. The first fatty arrived just after me and thumped himself down with a force that catapulted me at least a foot in the air, then, to my incredulous amazement, the other one came lumbering down the aisle, crushed four of my toes, and plummeted down in the seat on the other side of me. It was a horrendously painful but hilarious experience. I was encased in 1000 pounds of blubber. It overflowed from both sides like some obscene animated jelly. I sort of struggled up for air and remained there floating in mid space, rolling from side to side with every twitch or cough from the two Pavarottis, my bottom not even touching the seat. I hovered there trying desperately to keep my balance, terrified that if I slid to one side I would be engulfed like an amoeba having its lunch. Then the opera started and it was in German. German! I'm surprised the singers weren't all still trapped at the traffic lights. As the cacophony raised to an appalling climax the fatty on my left raised a ham like hand, pushed himself in the stomach and released a thundering, gusty fart. He turned his sweaty face to me, tapped the side of his nose and said conspiratorially: 'It must be the fried eggs!' Information that I was pleased to receive because this is an effect that I am unused to from fried eggs. He then belched, a pleasurable belch that went on for nearly as long as the German song on stage. 'How many fried eggs did you have?' I almost shrieked through the combination of noxious gases. 'Ooo, only about a dozen,' he reassured me. I decided that I needed an early night and abstracted myself from the clinging morass and made for the exit. I swear that as I struggled free there came a loud report like a cork from a champagne bottle...but I might have been mistaken, it could have been my flatulent acquaintance getting rid of the effects of yet one more fried egg.

    The second day started off a little better, I had breakfast early (avoiding at all costs the fried eggs) then went and joined the party visiting the wildlife park. This isn't the sort of thing I'm usually keen on but it seemed the best way to see all the relevant animals and saw them I did: kangaroos and wombats and koala. None of them particularly filled me with great enthusiasm watching these bored animals in such an unnatural habitat. A wild life park here doesn't engender the same feelings as at home, it's more of a sort of bomb site with a few bits of scrubby grass. Next a somewhat soiled man showed us how to make damper bread and billy tea things that I am convinced will be invaluable to know if ever I happen to be stuck in the Australian outback. When they all went off to throw a boomerang I sneaked away and took a taxi back to the ship.

    I went and fetched my swimming stuff and nipped into the kitchens to see Noor and offered to show her how to make damper bread and billy tea. She didn't seem that enthusiastic but she found me a bit of food anyway: a foot of French loaf, a slab of Brie and some grapes. Then I went off to hire a bicycle. Seriously, I fancied a bike ride, it's not the same cycling in the gym. This turned out to be more difficult than I thought, everybody was only too keen to rent me a car or a motorbike but a bike…? At last I was directed to a dirty little man in a dirty little shed who, when he finally understood what I wanted disappeared for about ten minutes then came back wheeling one of those upright monstrosities you see policeman riding in the World War Two movies. He beamed at me proudly and gestured invitingly towards this rusting heap. I eyed it uneasily then taking a deep breath I lunged at it, threw one leg over and after a gargantuan push by the dirty little man I was off. As I careered off down the rather steep hill I realised that the saddle was not ideal, not only was it much too high but it also had the unusual attribute of swinging wildly from side to side. Now, ideal though this feature may be in a rotating gun turret it is less than useful in a bicycle. So, I shot off down the hill at about Mach 2 occasionally giving one of the pedals a push when it flashed past, then I would swing wildly around on the merry-go-round like saddle and have another stab at the opposing pedal. And then the music started to play, the bike was louder than the last Harley I rented, hell it was louder than jet fighter turning on its afterburners! The overriding noise sounded remarkably like that time when I had tried to liquidize the cheese grater (I was slightly off my trolley at the time) but there was the more regular sounds coming from the pedals themselves both of which were bent inwards and caught the frame every time they went around. ***Futonk*** went the one, ***Futank*** went the other while the wheels added a further: ***Squigy, Squigy, Squigy*** every time I tried to apply the brakes. As I hurtled through the centre of Sydney I passed Summer and Sheena from the theatre group on board. 'Cool bike Nick,' shouted Summer. 'My Granddad's got one just like that,' howled Sheena. ***Futonk Futank, Futonk Futank… Squigy, Squigy, Squigy*** went I.

    My destination was Bondi Beach which is some way outside Sydney but with perseverance and a great deal of comment from rather rude Australians I finally made it. This is, of course, one of the most famous beaches in the world and it is huge and the sea is great but on the whole it is wearing a bit tatty. There are toilets and changing areas and all of them needed a good coat of paint, but the sand was fine. I got talking to a young American couple, Brad and Babs (sounds like a magician and his assistant) who were very nice. I shared my lunch with them and then we took it in turns to use their two surf boards. They were camping and had all their stuff with them so one of us would keep an eye on it while the other two would go surfing. I use the term surfing in its loosest sense when it comes to me. I've always considered it a over rated sport, or more likely, one of those sports that are only enjoyable when you are good at them. You lie on the board and paddle out into the sea, this takes hours and hours and hours. Then you wait for another interminable length of time for a good wave and when it comes you always choose the wrong one. Then you climb up on your board and immediately fall off. Then you do it all over again. Still, it was nice to tell everybody back on the ship that I had been surfing on Bondi Beach, they weren't that impressed though, everybody wanted to talk more about my cycling experience.

20 Hobart

Now, I'll tell you a secret, I didn't know where Tasmania was! Apparently, it's this huge island just off Australia. I was lying in bed thinking about **Futonging** and **Futanging** and fried eggs when Lito came in bearing his tray. I usually have cereal and croissants and honey and coffee and fruit…that sort of thing but every now and then he ignores my order and brings me something entirely different. I never acknowledge that he's done this so he is tending towards the more and more outrageous. Anyway, today it was a bowl of muesli, a yogurt, a mango and four pork sausages. He unloaded all this crap onto my side table but with a preoccupied air. 'Ooo, sah, there are many people wait for you at side of ship,' he said. 'Many people?' I demanded, thinking police? Army? The Poison Dwarf's legal firm? 'Lots of small girls,' Lito explained, 'hundreds of small girls, sah.' 'Oh cock,' said I knowingly, 'there aren't hundreds of small girls on Tasmania and if there were they wouldn't be waiting for me.'

But, you know what, they were! Well, not hundreds, 24 to be precise. What it was that my books **Crackling Ice** and **Skating on the Edge** had come out in Tasmania only six months before and one little girl had loved them (yes, a fan letter came flooding in) and she had started her whole school reading them and they had formed a fan club. A fan club? Me? Somehow they had found out I was visiting and had all come out to greet me. When I went ashore they all cheered, I hung around hoping that someone from the QE2 would notice but everywhere was deserted so I couldn't try out my modest smile. It was a really nice experience, a bit unreal, I mean it was only me, but nice. They all escorted me to their school and there was a big, life-size cardboard figure of the two characters off the front cover of **Crackling Ice** standing pride of place in the library. Where on Earth did they get it from? I can't imagine why anyone would even produce such a thing, surely not Pan Macmillan? I gave one of my talks and urged them all not to do any homework that night, I always love the look on the teachers' faces when I say that. Then I did a workshop session in one of the English classes, do you know they are even doing one of my books in class? Then I had school lunch which was somewhat different from the QE2 lunch then after signing about 50 autographs (me, an autograph? That's another first!) I was escorted back to the ship.

A really good day, especially for my ego but who's going to believe it back on board? The only thing wrong was that I hadn't actually seen any of Tasmania apart from the inside of a school and the ship was leaving in two hour's time. I waited until the little girls had gone then rushed out onto the quay and offered a taxi driver called Ian fifty pounds to show me as much of Tasmania as he could in two hours. Hobart's another great big city, very like all the rest but Tasmania's the Australian's Majorca and it's wonderful. I'd say it was one of the prettiest places the cruise has been. Ian turned into a friend, a really nice bloke and there was no hidden agenda because there isn't any tipping in the antipodes and what a refreshing idea that is. We drove around for about an hour and then Ian said I had to taste Tasmanian beer and took me to his favourite bar. It was only then I found out he is a polio cripple with two very wasted legs and what a good job taxi driving is for him. I had to help him into the bar and he insisted on buying the first pint. Now, I don't like beer and my head for drink is about the same as a budgerigars but I could hardly say no. Then, of course, I had to buy a round and then, for some reason, the barman had to get one in. Then I think we all went around again but things have grown a little hazy here. The last thing I remember was when Ian was showing me how he could steer the taxi with his feet even at 60 mph and then two big strong Cunard security men were helping me to my cabin…oh dear!

21 Melbourne

Ardy has become my friend. We started dancing together at dance class and we are both very forgiving and spend most of the time laughing. She's about 60 with six children and is a rich American, though when I introduce her as that she gets annoyed. She admitted that after the first evening at my table, when I had been having one of my long arguments with Arletta, she had gone to the restaurant manager and asked to change tables. He smiled and advised her to give it a few days. Well, now we discuss each other's love lives and other sundry problems and she is being bothered by this older man who keeps propositioning her in the most crude manner. His first chat up line with her was: 'Come back to my cabin with me, we're both old and fat but we can put the pillows down on the floor and I'll get on top!' As I said to Ardy, very Cary Grantish! She asked me to warn him off so I went to the ballroom with her and took him aside and very politely warned him off, he asked me to offer Ardy his apologies, all very civilised after all he was Italian. Ardy has been trying to get me to come dancing with her in the ballroom so there wasn't really any escape, not that I mind dancing with Ardy, we know each other's steps but the trouble is there are so many more women than men that you really are forced to ask others to dance. I asked this young Japanese woman to dance the Cha Cha with me and she was delighted because she hadn't been on the floor all night. I think she must have been some sort of professional back home because, bloody hell, she was good. It was like pushing a helium balloon around the floor.

Well, we've got quite friendly. Now, I'm not mad keen on the Japanese as a whole but I've decided to forget my prejudices for the duration. I've chosen this course in the cause of international harmony between nations, the growing sense of forgiveness throughout the world for the excesses in the last war…and because she is very pretty. She calls me Nick-Nick-Ha! No mere words can convey how sweet this sounds in real life but I'll have a go: The Nick-Nick is very fast and staccato like a horse race commentator presenting The Grand National while the Ha is very long and drawn out like the wind sighing through the trees on a balmy sunlight day. I'm not sure she isn't laughing at me because she always follows it up with a giggle. Her name is Sootu but I've no idea how it is spelled: Sue Two, Sutu, whatever, because she doesn't speak a word of English (the cheek of it!). I, however, had to know nearly 1000 Japanese words to get my black belt at karate so we should be okay. Unfortunately she doesn't understand a single word…not a bloody word! Obviously the Japanese we are taught in the martial arts is some Anglified crap taken from a dictionary. Sootu does have a friend who is articulate so occasionally we search her out to translate. She listens to Sootu intently then translates it into English at about 200mph with a strong Japanese accent. I can't understand a single word and so I always just nod when she has finished whereupon everybody present breaks out into another round of giggles.

I'm still seeing hairy Carol but she is getting pushy. Last night she came to dance wearing a nightie, I suspected some deliberate purpose but Paula assured me that it is just her getting mixed up again. However, there is nothing mixed up at the end of the night when I escort her back to her cabin and she keeps trying to get me inside, I should cocoa, I'd need to take my razor along! I stand in the lift doors, stopping them closing, while she stands invitingly in her cabin door trying to look alluring…ooo, it's ghastly. No, that's not fair, she's not that bad. Not really. She told Ardy, who she has obviously met, that I'm very shy, when Ardy told me this she had to have three goes at it.

So I took Sootu into Melbourne with me. I think the best description I can give is Dustin's (a South African blonde who works in the Lido restaurant): it's just one more big city. And I'm all citied out. We took the bus into the centre and went around the modern art gallery, which was very disappointing. There was a good Andy Warhol (that's a bit of an oxymoron) and a bad De Kooning which was a pity. Then we walked down the main street which is called Collins Street and is about three miles long and it's very hot. We sat and had coffee, I don't know whether Sootu likes coffee but like I say she doesn't speak the language so I just tend to order. And just when I thought the day a total frost, along he came…a man with a triangular head! Seriously, we are talking isosceles here. It was incredible, I swear it was perfect, Pythagoras could have proved his theorem on it. What made it even worse was that he had grown a horrible little beard on the point which made it look rather like someone had dipped a road warning sign in a tin of black treacle. We sat and drank him in until he disappeared from sight then we both heaved a sigh of contentment in unison. Well, after that nothing could top the day so I asked Sootu what she thought and she said: 'Hakka chakka, nakka, pana, pana, blamp.' So we went back to the ship for lunch and a swim. The last was a mistake because all the old biddies are used to watching in admiration as I do my 100 lengths but Sootu thinks she's Mark bloody Spitz! You know in war films when you see a submarine launch a torpedo at a battleship? It leaves a white trail in the water, well, that's Sootu swimming a length, she never even comes up for air.

There are other things though that make her sweet, for instance, I've always wondered how you take a girl to bed when you don't speak her language, well this turns out to be surprisingly easy though good taste means you will have to find this out for yourself. But, there is one thing I will share, the very last thing a Japanese woman does before she pulls the sheet back and climbs in beside you is to give a cute little bow. Now, I'm well used to woman bowing to me after we have been to bed, but before?

22 Adelaide

      Well, well, well! Remember about my invite to the Captain's table, and me turning him down? Well, the other morning the phone by the bed went right in the middle of my afternoon nap. I snatched it up and snapped into it a little frostily and a very posh lady asked if I would like to come to a small private dinner party with the Captain and his wife in their quarters. My steward would escort me there and back and there would be cocktails first and during dinner we would be entertained by Marie, the lady harpist. I had to say yes to that one and boy has it caused a fuss! Apparently these dinner parties are famous and very exclusive, as one old lady said to me: 'I've been around the world eleven times on this ship and I've never been invited to one.' So, you see, it pays to be arrogant at times.

      Lito came to fetch me and off I trolled in my white DJ. It was alright, both Big C and his lovely Hawaiian wife were very nice to me. There were only a handful of guests there but Big C spent the whole time talking to me. He is trying to be a writer, in fact he has written a history of the QE2 which they sell aboard (but nowhere else) and he is very interested in any information on how to get published. His wife was even more interested in karate, apparently she is a green belt back in Honolulu. Then we all went into dinner, it was all very dignified: 'Gentlemen, the Queen,' all that kind of thing. I expect the food was wonderful, I certainly thought it should be exhibited in the Tate Modern! It was so a la carte that it was unidentifiable and we had to be told what it was by the waitresses. Apparently, we had: warm fillet of turbot on a puree of green peas, peach sorbet, duck pieces in a white wine sauce with kumquats and some sort of puddingy thing that involved pears, raspberries and choux pastry. When we were finished we were all starving. The problem was that Dorcus was serving. She was thrilled to see me there and kept making little asides in my ear as she served me… 'Your Turbot sir…you pretentious shit,' and, 'another slice of pear flan…if your trousers can take the strain.' The problem was that I was trying to charm the Captain's wife at the time and kept spluttering into my handkerchief, she must have thought I was epileptic or something.

     On the whole a good experience but I missed my usual dinner companions and after it finished I went to the dining room and joined them for coffee, well, more to swank about my private dinner really. There was a real barmpot sitting in my usual place so I had to pull up an extra chair by Ardy. She rolled her eyes in the barmpot's direction and I studied him closely but he seemed quite normal for QE2 standards and then he suddenly sprang to his feet like a Russian gymnast sitting on a hatpin.

Immediately he launches into Shakespeare's **Friends, Romans and Countrymen** speech. Apparently he does this all the time, so much so that the waiters and the people on his usual table don't bat an eye, just ignore him. Well, he sits down again and goes on munching through his desert of luxury Black Forest Gateau. The coffee comes and he's off again but this time I am ready and as he rockets upwards so do I and I give everybody the **Double Double** speech from Macbeth. This time, because it isn't the barmpot, everybody loves it and I get a huge round of applause from everybody including the serving staff. The barmpot, who has been completely drowned out by my voice takes umbrage and storms off in a huff. Apparently, he told Arletta, who had invited him onto the table, that he would never join us for dinner again…sad!

Adelaide is very nice indeed. I thought I'd had enough of cities but Adelaide is okay, it has a lot more charm than most of the others. The city is exactly one mile square and can never get any bigger because it is set in a square of greenbelt. This means space is at a premium and every new building has to be built on the site of an old one and you get some rather odd compromises. I took Sootu ashore with me and we sat outside in the main shopping mall and I had my first iced coffee and some cream-cheese filled pancakes to go with it. Heaven only knows what Sootu had, ooo, she eats some crap! She eats raw fish, I mean really eats it. I thought it was just something Marks and Spencer's put on to look posh, or that it was something you use to threaten your kids with: 'If you don't behave I'm going to make you eat some raw fish!' And the soup she pours down herself, it looks like washing up water with great white lumps in it…I reckon its got bits of dead people in it. It kinda puts you off, I mean, you go to kiss her then you remember where her mouth has been…ugh! I've developed this strategy with Sootu as she can't talk, I've taught her to say absolutely. Well, to be more accurate it is more: absworootly. Anyway, I talk to her at great length about any subject in the world from politics to Garibaldi biscuits while she sits there with this slightly puzzled expression on her face staring at me with those almond eyes. When I finally run down and pause, I give her a nod and she comes right in with her absworootly. It's a perfect arrangement.

We went to the art gallery and it was the best collection I have seen this whole trip. There was this wonderful collage of literally hundreds of tiny framed old photographs of people set in a circle which surprised me by being amazing. The only disappointment was there was this big sign up: **Modern Australian Women** but when I asked at the kiosk they hadn't got any. I went shopping and found a tiny mirror for my bike helmet that I had searched for all over Britain and America and I bought Sootu a pair of white jeans which two assistants had to help her into and it still took over five minutes, but she wore them back to the ship and it was worth it. The only problem was that there was an Australian bagpipe band in the Grande Lounge so we went to the other end of the ship so we could do some work, well, I was typing away while Sootu just sort of leaned against the table as she couldn't actually sit down in her new jeans. Then this bloody band follows us and stops at my table and does this appalling version of *Waltzing Matilda.* Can you imagine? *Waltzing Matilda* is bad enough normally, but *Waltzing Matilda* on the bagpipes? I nearly lost my cream cheese pancakes. And the very worst thing of all is that when they finished

we had to pretend to give them enthusiastic applause, personally I think that the only thing which would make them sound tolerable is a few blasts from a double barrelled shotgun. I'll leave the last word to Sootu: 'Inewaquie pang pang.'
    Abswerootly!

23 Perth

You really begin to understand just how big Australia is when you cruise around it. The cities where everybody but Crocodile Dundee lives are so far apart that we have a full day and night at sea between visits. This is good because as I have said before you don't actually look forward to the stops, it's the life aboard that you enjoy the most…well, it rather depends on the state of your relationships I suppose.

I've got a sort of loose relationship with three woman on board, not counting Ardy who knows about all three and is vastly amused by the antics I go through to keep them apart. Well, last night my absolute worst scenario actually happened and I'm not totally convinced that Ardy wasn't behind it! I'm still seeing hairy Carol, I've taken to meeting her in the disco because Sootu is usually in the ballroom and we still get to dance the tango there. So there we are at about 11.30 dancing away when I feel another woman alongside and as we are the only one's on the dance floor I gallantly extend my dancing to include her only to find that it's Sootu. Imagine, me dancing with the two woman I most want to keep apart in the whole world…it couldn't get any worse. Oh yes it could! The next thing that happened was that Daniella went past, now Daniella is one of my cheering section and I count her as a friend but she is also Paula's best friend. She gave a double take at me dancing with the two woman and I gave an airy wave. She waved back then disappeared and only seconds later Paula erupted onto the dance floor. Damn, she looked good, she was wearing this long flowing orange dress right to the floor with the same material hanging from her arms and a low neckline showing off her suntan. I can't imagine why she hasn't been snapped up for a film role, she makes Angelina Jolie look like a dog. So, we've got Paula floating around the floor like some orange goddess, then there's Sootu, much smaller, but looking good enough to eat dressed in a sort of white kimono thing doing a kind of reggae step. Lastly, there's Carol, the lighting hiding her hairs, dressed in a slinky black number that metamorphoses into see-through lace around her legs, and she's dancing all romantic movements up real close. So there was Nick dancing with one then the other, then, well, you get the picture. The problem was when I was dancing with one the other two were dancing with each other and woman can't do anything without talking though how they communicated with Sootu is beyond me, perhaps it's some woman's thing? Then when their turn with me came they would interrogate me. This was the kind of dialogue that took place:

> Carol, 'I didn't know that you knew Paula?'
> Me, 'Oh, didn't I tell you?'
> Carol, 'No you did not! Did you know she was one of my best friends?'
> Me, (darkly) 'Oh good.'
> Paula, 'I didn't know you knew Carol?'
> Me, 'Oh, didn't I tell you?'
> Paula, 'No, you did not. We're best of friends, we tell each other everything!'
> Me, (darkly) 'Oh good.'
> Sootu, 'Chakki hakki penakki bang.'
> Me, 'Abswerootly.'

I promise that all the above is absolutely accurate. I didn't get away until gone three and I was so soaked with sweat that I had to send my entire evening wear away to be dry cleaned. I'm thinking of killing myself in the morning.

    I crept off the ship at Freemantle avoiding all feminine company half thinking of staying there permanently, the idea of facing any of the three women horrifies me, I honestly don't know how these philanderers cope. Freemantle, (Freo is the in thing to call it) is just the port for Perth which is ten miles away. The interesting thing about Perth is that it is completely isolated so you get this huge modern city with great shining glass skyscrapers right in the middle of nowhere. Adelaide is three days away on the train, so if you can't get something in the city you've had it. Like the other Australian cities Perth is a self-contained colony with its own colleges, universities, law courts prisons…everything, even a medial school! I was driven there by a taxi driver who didn't speak at all but kept breaking wind virtually non stop, and I mean non stop. And loudly…and with no sense of embarrassment at all. There's a fuel saving option open to him there, if he can find a way of connecting his bottom up to the engine he'd never have to buy petrol again. When I got out I thanked him for the air conditioning.

    I walked around, had lunch (three ice creams) then bored I took a taxi back, firstly having a good sniff in the back before risking it. This time I lucked out, the driver was an ex-Bosnian, he'd been a minor politician back home and when they'd murdered his father and burnt his house down he took the remains of his family and fled to Perth. I never asked him why out of all the places in the world to go he had chosen Perth, it just didn't seem polite. He was a really nice bloke and didn't break wind once that I could tell and he took me for a ride around the city pointing out all the places of interest before dropping me off at the ship and charging me half of what the farter had charged. Serindipa (that's what it sounded like) said that this was the happiest time of his life.

Well, that was the end of Australia and I've got to say how impressed I was. The cities are all new and shining, the green belt is great and the people all very friendly. In spite of all I had heard I didn't meet a single Australian who was rude to me, even the farting taxi driver was a black immigrant. I just feel that if I lived there I would get the feeling of isolation I got when I lived in Cornwall.

24 Bali

My social life has become less complicated by a third, Sootu got off at Bali. She woke me up at six in the morning, a feat indeed, just to see her off. She's been practicing some English phrases to say goodbye to me properly for over a week now, our interpreter told me this in between giggles. So we stood at the top of the gangplank waiting for the tender to finally dock and I swear there were tears in her eyes, (though it might have been the wind 'cos it was blowing something cruel) and I was thinking: **Get a blasted move on will you, I want to get back to bed!** She turned to me in what was to be our final moment together, held my hand tightly, and very carefully said, 'Onion paggi in England one one!' And do you know I really think she meant it!

I had a long lie in then made my way ashore to see: **This jewel in the crown of the Southern Seas,** and **the most attractive South Sea island.** Or so the cruise guide would have us believe. Well, if it is I might as well go home right now. I mean, it's okay with mountains and forests and beaches and that kind of stuff but it also has too many people and scraggy dogs and scraggy monkeys, and too much traffic and too much pollution. I can't really see what the whole of America seems to rave about, Hawaii is ten times better. The street traders have to be experienced to be believed, you have to shoulder them aside to make any progress at all. Now, this is no great problem because they are a very small people but some of the more timid passengers simply got straight back on the ship. The prices are unbelievable: four T shirts $5, intricate woodcarvings $1, CD player batteries $2 for 100.

    I rented a proper motorbike, an almost new Kawasaki 350 only $10 for eight hours. How is that possible unless he stole it? And how do you steal a damn great motorbike on a tiny island like Bali? Off I roared, ooh, I did look good. I did a half sort of wheelie in front of a bunch of the crew and got a round of applause off them (I didn't actually mean to do a wheelie of course but the truth is that I have hardly ever ridden a motorbike before this cruise and the clutch was a bit stiff). The first thing of interest I found is a massive cage full of bats and as I have always wanted to be David Attenborough I stopped. The guide was thrilled to have a potential customer so I gave him a dollar to leave me alone and wandered around occasionally stamping a foot to get them to fly about. But standing in a rain of bat shit palls after a time so off I went again. I went around the whole island, I visited the temples and the beaches and all the time I was getting more and more confident on this bike. Heading back I fell into this race with this Chinese man and we hurtled off across the island on what was purported to be the main road. He was a much better rider than me so he went around bends better but my Kawasaki was much more powerful so I would catch him up on the straights. He took me through a village scattering hens everywhere, then up a hill and down another one and then all of a sudden there was this bloody hairpin bend. He leaned right over and went around it like Barry Sheene. I leaned over and went around it like Barry

White. Oh shit did I come a cropper! I did about 100 yards on my side, sparks flying everywhere as I slid relentlessly into the path of this oncoming lorry. Then I finally grated to a halt and all I could see was this huge tyre coming straight for my head. I gave a convulsive jerk out of the way and saw the wheel inch past, the wheel arch went right over me. Then all was peace and I was still alive. The bloody Chinese man had vanished into the blue and apart from blowing his horn the lorry driver did nothing, just roared off down the hill belching smoke. But I was still in the middle of a busy road so I staggered to my feet and hauled the motorbike to the side and sat down for a bit of a think.

      There was blood all down my one side and I was sure I had dislocated my shoulder, but I couldn't afford to, I had ridden past the hospital on my island tour and there was no way I was going to stay there. Somehow, I managed to get back on the bike and gingerly set off back to the ship at about five miles an hour. The man who hired the bike wasn't too happy with his nearly new bike which now had a bent pedal and scratches all down one side. I didn't feel like being too sympathetic so I threw him another $10 and staggered back onto the ship and hid in my safe little cabin. Carefully I undressed to view the damage, I hadn't dared to earlier or I might not have made it back. I put on my dressing gown and limped up to the medical room where the South African doctor looked after me, sadly the nurse wasn't there but my libido was at a very reduced level so it didn't matter that much. I'd got 19 abrasions, some in places you wouldn't believe, I'd pulled all the tendons in my shoulder and my legs were so blue with bruises they looked like I'd been in a traffic accident. And, boy! Did I feel lucky? No, not really, if I was lucky I wouldn't have fallen off the bloody thing in the first place. There was nothing wrong with me that a few days wouldn't put right but the main problem was that I felt in need of some tender loving care and all the staff were spending the night ashore in a hotel. Sootu had gone, Paula was ashore and so was hairy Carol…if she wasn't I'd even have risked visiting her cabin, even she wouldn't think of me doing anything active injured as I am.

25 Manila

I borrowed a stick from the quack and limped upstairs to the Red Lion. It was auction day so all my cheering section were there and they were so concerned that it was almost worth the accident. Actually I'm not as bad as I thought I would be, my legs are a bit stiff and my shoulder won't be doing pull ups for a while but I've had worse after a row with the Poison Dwarf. They all sat with me and bought me coffee and bagels and they were all very feminine and nice…I really do like women more than men.

Then they told me about this new passenger who had come aboard at Melbourne. He's a Spaniard with a very short temper. Apparently he loses it at the slightest excuse, a very nice American lady accidentally touched him with her handbag in the lift and he exploded and kept on bawling at her until he had left her trembling. Then there's this elderly man who staggered into him when we were in a rough sea and you could hear him two decks below. As for the waitresses on his table he never stops on at them until he has reduced them to tears. My cheering section wouldn't point him out to me because they said I was injured and anyway was still getting over my breakdown and might overreact. Me? Overreact? So I asked Ardy and of course she knew who he was (women always know everything when it concerns other people) and she pointed him out to me. And, do you know, it was uncanny but I bumped into him three times today that same day: by the swimming pool, the Lido and once I kicked his chair in the dining room, and he hasn't said a thing. I think my accident must leave me looking a bit liverish. The following morning, though, my relationship with him deteriorated, for no real reason he went off like an H bomb when we were both getting into the lift. I couldn't understand it, all I did was stand in his way while everybody else got in first and it only seemed practical to put my hand on his chest to stop him getting bumped. Boy, I saw what they meant, he went bright scarlet and started howling at me like a gorilla. I couldn't quite make out what he was saying because it was mainly in Spanish but it definitely seemed less than polite, but the thing that I disliked the most was that he thrust his great sweaty face right into mine as he said it. There's this thing I do when people offer me violence, I put my hand in their faces and push them away, (I got it off Big Daddy the wrestler who used to do it in the ring) it cuts all the threats and talking out, they either start hitting me or back off. Well, he sort of ended up pressed against the back wall of the lift with me standing up very close giving him a friendly smile. Well, to be totally honest it was more of a glare than a friendly smile, I used to practice it in the mirror to use on karate opponents in the ring. We went right down five floors then up again and he didn't even try to budge an inch. Then I decided it was time to break the ice so I said, 'Now, I'm going to try very hard, but I don't think I'm going to like you.' I gave him a friendly smile and limped off to the Lido for lunch.

And even this was a problem, to reach the Lido you have to pass the library and after the disco I really didn't fancy the confrontation with the hairy one so I had to sort of creep past. Ardy has sworn she hasn't told anyone about my disco debacle but the whole ship knows and all my dining table companions had promised to be in the ballroom on the night to see what develops…bastards! It was the Valentine's ball and I had promised to take Carol and everybody knew this so I couldn't back out so I dumped me stick, put on my DJ and strolled off to the library to pick her up. She was sitting, waiting, dressed up like a ballerina so I casually took her by the arm and escorted her to the Queen's Ballroom. It was all going so well, Carol hadn't said a thing about Paula or Sootu, and everybody was watching and feeling snaped then the bloody compere had to announce a taxi dance: 'The next is a taxi dance, this is where the gentlemen keep changing ladies…if any of you are not too sure of how to do this watch Nick Walker here, he's an expert at it!' Now, I thought that this was funny, I still do. The crowd thought it was hilarious but Carol was furious and stormed off. I spent the rest of the night dancing with Ardy so it wasn't all a waste.

The next morning we berthed at Manila. This isn't a tourist spot by a long way but most of the Filipino staff are from here so they get a chance to visit their families and unload all the stuff they have accumulated on their travels. You wouldn't believe what they have bought or won or stolen: televisions, dishwashers, washing machines all the stuff you wouldn't dream of having in your luggage, this is nothing to them, they just bribe it through the customs.

Most of the passengers stay aboard because Manila is supposed to be one of the biggest slums in the world: the traffic is terrifying, the pollution unbelievable, the street traders and the prostitutes unrelenting, the muggers almost as common as the rats, the shops filthy, the crowds crushing…I liked it! I really did. Perhaps it was because my expectations were nil but it has a kind of bustling cheerfulness which comes from the Filipinos themselves who are a cheerful, happy people whom seem contented with their lot. I've never seen so many shop assistants in my life, they go around in fours and they are all exactly the same, like clones. When you see four of them bearing down on you all wearing the same identical clothes and the same identical smile it's like you are not yet recovered after a particularly heavy drinking session. The clothes are all tiny because they are such a small people and the dogs are all scraggy and starving. I pushed one off that was attempting to have sex with my leg (a dog that is not a Filipino) and a man shouted at me and came storming up, 'No! No! No!' he roared and I thought, 'Hello, we're going to have a bit of a confrontation here,' but no he came and booted the dog up it's arse so hard it must have landed two streets away.

    Actually, I don't have to describe Manila any further, all you have to do is to watch ***Apocalypse Now*** (my least favourite film…it's probably more fun to fly there and back to Manila) and it's exactly the same which is hardly surprising because that's where it was filmed.

26 Kobe

I was going into dinner when I was attacked by this old man of 80. It came as a bit of a surprise, there are signs for the restaurants, the bars, the cinema, the shops, the rest rooms, the theatre, even the bridge, but nowhere are there any signs warning you of 80 year-old muggers working the dining room! He sort of leaped out at me from behind a

Filipino restaurant manager and started belabouring me with his library book (John Grisham's **The Rainmaker**). It's surprisingly difficult to defend yourself against an old man of 80, I mean you can hardly go hitting him can you and even if you try to block the rain of blows you are worried about fracturing his arm or something. Soon, though, he ran out of breath and had to have a sit down to recuperate…presumably for an attack on his next victim. His daughter, who I might add stood calmly by as he beat me up, apologised in a peremptory kind of fashion and said I reminded him of someone he had been in the navy with during the last war, apparently he had a beard too. She gave me a knowing nod of dismissal and led her father away. I got the feeling that she was expecting me to shave my beard off!

    I was dining early because I thought I had found a way out of my dilemma. I'd got a firm date with Carol so I stood her up and went to see Gerry and the Pacemakers instead. They were good, excellent, in fact! Fat little Gerry is an ageing icon but he has some smashing songs still. Afterwards, Dustin (the South African Blonde) smuggled me through the crews quarters to avoid the ballroom so I could get to my work desk by The Lido. Guess who was sitting in my chair dressed up to the nines? What does that expression mean? Where exactly are the nines? Somewhere high up on your body and does this mean that above the nines you are not done up at all? Anyway, the upshot of the short, but interest-filled scene with Carol that followed is that we are going dancing together tomorrow…and no, even I wouldn't dare!

    Japan? Well, it's very Japanese. And that's another thing, why didn't Sootu get off here? Why Bali? Perhaps it's because she's inscrutable, or is that just the Chinese?

The best way I can describe Japan is that it is very like walking through a Dixon's catalogue. It was also surprisingly tatty…and that's just the people! I mean, I didn't like the Japanese before Sootu then I was sort of ambivalent about them but after Kobe I certainly didn't like them again. Everybody just walks through you, even the women, who are supposed to be subservient, just shoulder you aside. It's a problem, how do you know that the arrogant little shit who pushes you into the gutter isn't a master at some obscure martial art who is able to execute you with just his thumb? And another thing, do you know that the arrogant bastards don't speak English? I think it's disgusting, where would we be if we all refused to learn each other's languages? It shows lack of tolerance. They do have one good idea that I feel we should immediately adopt for certain members of out society, a lot of them wear facemasks. There's a Korean woman on board who would certainly be improved by the addition of one.

    Japan is ludicrously expensive. I found my camera here, the place of its birth, 100 pounds dearer. Ardy told me, that evening at dinner, that she had paid $98 for a tour: they went up a mountain but it was foggy so they came back down again, had a glass of sake then came back to the ship…I envy her, she had more fun than me!

    Actually Ardy is a real laugh, she is on her own so she usually goes on a tour whenever we go ashore. The best bit is that she has the most amazing talent, no matter how many tours are offered she always manages to pick the real duff one. At friendly Jamaica (while I was being mugged) she went to have an old-fashioned high tea at an old-fashioned tea planter's mansion. She had us in stitches when she related the three-hour drive over rutted roads to finally arrive at a falling down ruin of a house. After banging on the door for some ten minutes the falling down tea planter finally opened it roaring drunk. He bellowed at them then herded them into the filthy lounge like they were cattle and ordered a haggard old woman to wait on them. After an interminable wait, while he sat on the couch glaring at them and picking his teeth, the haggard old woman returned bearing some luke warm tea and some cakes that looked like something King Alfred had cooked. Then the tea planter fell asleep and started to snore like an elephant. But, Ardy persisted, worse was to come, in between cavernous snores the tea planter commences to fart, long, melodious smelly gusts of wind that she swears they could actually feel. They crept out so as not to wake him and made their getaway while the haggard old woman shouted abuse at them from the balcony. When they complained the Cunard rep insisted that it was one of their most popular tours.

    Then there was the ride on a sea plane in Perth. For some unexplained reason it couldn't get off the ground or sea, whatever. After innumerable attempts the pilot gave up and instead took them on a water tour by plane, roaring around the most boring port in the world. Guess what, sea planes aren't meant for this and have only little floats and soon the whole plane load (including the pilot) were throwing up all over the place.

    I try and get back early on these days and it was easy to tear myself away from Japan. It means I can slide into the computer room and print out my manuscripts in private. It's not that any of the staff will stop you, the staff are so meticulously trained in politeness that you feel you could stand on a table in the dining room and have a pee and all they would do is fetch you a very clean bucket. But it kinda feels wrong to print out great reams of paper when everybody else is just printing the single sheet and there's always a muttering queue when yours finishes. Today the bloody printer was jammed and I opened various little doors and pressed a multitude of buttons and little lights flashed at me but nothing else happened so I thumped it and finally lifted it up and dropped it and this fixed it properly. I set it printing and went off to do my Emails, well, I thought it was going on a bit but I wasn't really concentrating and when I returned it had printed out about ten copies of a 15,000 word manuscript. I only managed to stop it by removing all the paper. I crept away hugging enough paper to stock a small but vigorous school for a year. I spent the rest of the day typing in the Lido while they kept bringing around parties of jabbering Japanese tourists, I would be pointed out as a famous (sic) author and everybody would take photos of me…it's finally happened, I've become a tourist attraction.

    I know it's unbelievable but I rather appear to have got myself another date. It's with Muriel, the sommelier (no, no, the wine steward!). Only she is French and pronounces her name as Moo wee elle which makes you go weak at the knees. I was just chatting her up a bit, as you do, and she said she knew Hong Kong a bit and I naturally suggested she show me around and without even trying I found myself fixing up a date for the following day. I mean, I know she's French but she's French woman and that can't be all bad can it? She's 32 (it's getting better) and has the most wonderful hips and she doesn't seem at all hairy. Must remember to check under her arms!

27 Hong Kong

Well now, Hong Kong? It's a bit difficult to describe, it's very Hong Kongey. It's nothing like New York or London but some bits of it are very like New York and London, sometimes both at the same time. Midland Red double decker buses for instance, only they run in fours here because that is what Hong Kong is about: people! There are so many people it is unimaginable, it seems like at least 100 million Chinese live here all rushing about but then again everybody here rushes about all of the time. And queuing? We have no idea in Britain what queuing is! I took a picture of a four abreast queue that ran right around the block, I followed it hoping for something good and it turned out to be a cash dispenser. And they all move very fast, even check-out girls move in a kind of a blur. To see four of them pricing up a supermarket trolley has to be seen to be believed, it looks just like a cartoon where their arms and legs move in a blur.

  I took Mooweeelle ashore, or rather she took me and we did what the guidebook suggested and took the ferry to Hong Kong Island, a rickshaw to the bus station, a battered bus up the hill and the funicular railway to the top…it took two hours and cost over 100 pounds! The taxi ride home again took 15 minutes and cost under ten pounds...I wonder if the bloke who writes the guidebook is in league with the rickshaw drivers? The rickshaw drivers were a real trip, they insisted we took two and kept looking meaningfully at my waistline and Mooweeelle's hips so we climbed aboard hoping to experience the romanticism of the Far East. My rickshaw driver was an asthmatic toothless 80 year-old who kept gasping and groaning so much I nearly got out and pulled him. I was terrified he was going to have a heart attack and that I would have to give him mouth to mouth! Mooweeelle's driver was a skinny young man who looked like a prisoner from the Gulag, he was a real charmer who kept spitting at every other step, Moowieeelle swore that it was like being under a light but constant shower. They both stopped after 500 yards and charged us 12 quid each. Actually, it is a lot less fun than you think, all I felt was a feeling of acute embarrassment.

    The ferry in contrast was much more impressive: it comes hurtling into the berth bells ringing wildly and hoards of people pour off, the porters actually push the waiting passengers aboard with almost brutal force but it's forgivable because almost immediately the bells are ringing wildly and the boat is hurtling out again. All very efficient and after the QE2's constant **_Safety First_** crap a real refreshing change. The closest I can liken it to is one of those ski gondolas that only stop for five seconds and you have to be aboard and sitting down in that time...if you are one of those slow people who get on everybody's nerves then you'd never get off a Hong Kong ferry in a million years.

The funicular railway (is it me or does that sound rude to you: funicular?) had its moments: Mooweeelle had her bottom pinched. She gave a sort of half squeal then a little smile but refused to say what had happened till later. She confessed that she had kept it quiet in case I had done something about it. I actually have the most reverent admiration for the guy, never in my life have I had to nerve to pinch a strange woman's bottom and imagine doing it when she is with a man! Strangely Mooweeelle insists that it was a Frenchman who pinched it. I was fascinated by this, how could she tell? Apparently a bottom pinching Frenchman goes about it in a different manner to his European counterparts, when pressed Mooweeelle demonstrated on me, in an abandoned manner that harbours well for the future, a kind of stroking grope where the fingers more caress than pinch. I've been practising on a mango I got from the buffet ever since.

The best thing about Hong Kong is the view of Hong Kong you get from the top, but it's all money, money, money, don't believe what they say about it being cheap. Except for the tailors. Mooweeelle took me to one down a side street that she said I would like. I did as well, he was called Harry Fuck! Really, he had it emblazoned in neon lighting right across the road: ***Cum To Harry Fucks***! Then she suggested I went inside and challenged me not to buy anything, well, I'm the hero of Columbia, no slit- eyed sweaty little Chinese is going to intimidate me. I pushed the door open and my arm was slid into a shirt sleeve then a little man whipped around the back of me and slid it onto the other arm while another little man buttoned up the front. You've never seen anything so slick in your life! He said how was the shirt, I said I didn't like the colour, so he said what colour did I like and I said deep blue. Now I am the proud owner of two deep blue shirts. Suddenly I was being groped for the second time in less than an hour, another little man had his hand between my legs and yes really between them. I jumped and he said my inside leg was twenty eight inches, I said I was thrilled to know that, he said he had just the suit to fit, I said…oh well, to cut a long story short I am now the proud owner of a brilliant white suit made of cashmere (yeah, right!).

Mooweeelle was working that night so I slid ashore at about eleven and singled to a taxi. 'Susie Wong,' I said and he nodded and ten minutes later I was walking around Wain Chang the most famous red light district in the world. It's surprisingly small, Soho is huge by comparison. There seems to be few night clubs, the ones that are there have those nauseating pictures outside that would put me off women for life. The atmosphere is quite cheerful and little groups of prostitutes heckle you for business as you go by, if you laugh with them they laugh cheerfully back at your refusals. Now I've gone for a look, I have never paid for sex in my life but then again to be fair I have never charged for it either and to me making love to a stranger is something I can't imagine doing…anyway, what with Carol stalking me and Mooweeelle pinching my bottom I think I'm well fixed in that respect. So I was just walking around and suddenly there was this girl under my arm. She should have worked for Harry, it was so smooth it was like a conjuring trick. She must have been hidden in a doorway and ducked under my arm and suddenly she was there. 'Oh sar, I be very dirty girl for you all night long, 100 Hong Kong dollar.' That means that this divine, almond eyed creature had just offered to sleep with me for the whole night, indulging my every wicked whim for under ten pounds! I looked at her, she was about 14 years old, but with very lived in eyes…she could have been in my year 11 class back in Britain! "Young lady,' I said portentously, 'all you'll get from me is a good spanking.' She considered this for a long moment then said, 'Oh, then that will be 200 Hong Kong dollars!' (I had to play around with the actual dialogue to make that last line so funny.)

I think it's sad, all these lovely girls. I had been invited to the crew's party at an Irish pub in the middle of Rangoon (three times no less) and as both Carol and Mooweeelle are staff rather than crew, and Paula is rated a passenger, I felt it was safe to go along. I needed cheering up after my nightly excursion, it was the way that when I refused her she disappeared without looking back once, like a cat that has finished all the cream on your plate. The idea of what she must think of men, so the party was just what I needed: very common and very rough and very, very loud. I got back to the ship at gone four, I had intended to remain completely sober after that business in Tasmania but it simply isn't possible in an Irish pub with Irish amongst the crew members.

That was it for Hong Kong, a place everybody should visit at one time but where no one should ever live!

28 Vietnam

I've been having a little chuckle about Vietnam. Remember June and John? They're the couple who employed me to bodyguard them in Columbia. Well, June and me have got quite friendly, she often turns up at dance class sans John. Vietnam is seriously dodgy so they asked me to go with them. Saigon/Ho Chi Min city is 70 miles away and that is three hours each way by car or taxi but June has found out that it is only one and a half hours by hydrofoil, the trouble is that they only leave every two hours so I arranged to meet them on the hydrofoil at about seven the following morning.

 Then something strange happened, you know like my safe being searched on the first day aboard: The purser called for me to drop in and see him, this is something you don't refuse, he doesn't call you in for a chat about the weather. Apparently I had been refused permission to enter Vietnam, the only person on board to have their passport refused. No explanation, nothing. I mean, I can understand people who know me not wanting me in their country, but hell, we haven't even been introduced. The purser was very nice but he didn't want to discuss the matter at all. He told me that if I just wanted to visit the local area then I'd probably be okay but if I went into Saigon then I wouldn't be returning in the near future.

 Anyway, it was a relief, I woke up with a blinding headache, it might have been a hangover but I truly don't know what they feel like having never really got drunk since my teen years. It was six o clock so thankfully I went back to sleep only to be awakened by Lito with my breakfast who told me that the sea was too rough and that the trips ashore had been cancelled after the first boat ashore had nearly overturned. I went and had a look from the flat launching berth and the sea did have a big swell but there were bum boats all around trying to sell stuff. I called to one of them and he came in close then on an impulse, and because so many people were watching and I had my reputation to think of, I dived in and swam over to it (it was only about 20 yards away). Two very strong, wrinkled old woman scrambled me over the side and I gestured to the shore which was probably 200 yards away.

It was worth it because I got a round of applause from the watching passengers but the local village sure as hell wasn't worth visiting. It was a poor, ramshackled affair and everybody kept trying to sell me food, not prepared food but things like eggs and live chickens. The beach was okay, so I went for a stroll along it but the beggars still followed me all shouting at the top of their voices, I can't understand their thinking! If I'm not in the market to buy a live chicken then surely they realise no amount of shouting is going to change my mind!

I stayed ashore long enough to impress the passengers then I took the same boat back, they had stayed waiting ashore all that time. Getting aboard looked like it was going to be a problem because the water was really vigorous by this time but actually it was easy, I just slid over the side of the bum boat (after leaving all of my Vietnamese money with them), swam about two strokes and grabbed hold of the edge of the landing platform and as the water surged away I just did a smooth pull up and the stewards helped me to my feet. What was all the fuss about? Then I had a truly good day: I went and weight trained, had lunch in the Lido with my cheering section, avoided Carol, went for a swim (in the pool) in the afternoon and went to bed for a nap. On the night I joined my table for dinner then went to see an open air showing of **Anna and The King**, the new version of **The King and I**. It was fabulous, the stars had to be seen to be believed, the night sky was so huge that it frightened. We all sat in deck chairs on the top deck while the crew showed the movie on a flapping cloth screen, like in the old films. One of the chefs cooked us popcorn and a waitress served drinks. Wonderful, an unannounced item that wasn't in any program.

    June and John's day was a mite different! Not wanting to miss anything they were first in the queue for the shore tender at six o clock. This was the only tender to leave that day and the 200 yard journey to the shore took over two hours, no wonder Big C cancelled the rest. By the time they reached the shore everybody was wrackingly sick and pleading to be taken back to the ship but it was too rough to dock. Anyway, it wasn't all bad, they were still in time for the nine o clock hydrofoil. Lucky eh? No! After an hour up the coast it blew a fuse and they had to hike three miles to the nearest dirt road and wait three hours for a bus back to the ship. The bus abandoned them at the shoreline amongst the hoard of beggars I had experienced earlier in the day. It should have been alright, all they had to do was to get the tender back to the ship. Remember the tender that couldn't dock because the sea was too rough? Well, it was still too rough and they had to sit in the dirt from five pm until midnight in the most appalling conditions: the heat was intense, the humidity at a maximum, the beggars intimidating…the toilet was a hole in the ground where the beggars could cluster around to watch you commune with nature. Finally, it was judged that the sea was calm enough to travel and they had another dreadful journey back to the ship. They got back about one and I went to welcome them home and John called me a two-faced bastard, but his heart wasn't in it. June didn't say anything, she was too busy being sick over the side of the gangplank. I wanted to borrow their WAP phone tomorrow…perhaps in a few days.

29 Malaysia

I went to Bangkok in a taxi driven by a mad Elvis fan. The inside of his Toyota was completely plastered with magazine pictures of him. We had a great time, we sang to his Elvis tapes at the top of our voices all the way there and back, my voice was better than his (yes it was!). The journey was better than Bangkok. The Elvis lover took me to the temple and introduced me to the Buddhist priests. I got on quite well until I asked one of them who the statue of the fat chap was and he bowed very low and told me it was Buddha (I do wish I hadn't said fat now but then again he was fat if the statue is anything to go by). The temple was okay but sort of down a side street and apart from a pretty roof there was little enough to see. Then I asked for the toilets and was shown to a kind of hut and I have never seen anything so animalistic in my life, even a pack of hyenas would turn their nose up at this midden! I popped around the back for a pee, disgusted that any human beings could live like that…and this was the temple! We then went for a drive around but Bangkok is so big that there is no real centre so I strolled around a mall but it made me think I was back in London, everything is exactly the same. Soon there won't be any point in going abroad because everything will be the same wherever you go.

The following day wasn't the same though: I went to the local holiday town, Pappaya, or something like that.

It was a lot more fun than Bangkok, like Blackpool gone mad. I spent an hour in a bank trying to get some money, we think we have too much bureaucracy in the West but we're just pikers. The thing I can't get over is the way you just wander around inside, behind the tills and everywhere. Like Hawaii they refused to accept my driving license as it's an old one with no photo but they were quite happy to advance me $500 on the strength of my SCUBA diving card.

     Once again it was the prostitutes who were most evident, being a man on my own makes me a target and I began to realise what it is like being a woman in a Latin country. The girls all sit in the open air bars looking and giggling like schoolgirls and when I walked past they would all swoop across and lean over the wall shouting at me sounding like a flock of crows (yes, I do know that the correct collective noun is murder of crows but it sounds so damn silly). Then when I turned them down they would all cackle and swoop away like a black cloud back to their video games and music players. And they've taken prostitution mobile! One girl drives a motor scooter while another sits sideways on the back soliciting for custom, she even manages to keep crossing and re-crossing her legs without falling off. I saw a huge neon sign: **Blow Job $10,** rather sadly it turned out to be a hairdressers. But the thing that fascinated me most was the benches on the beach, these are about every 100 yards or so and standing motionless on each one was an elegant woman. You wouldn't believe them, they looked just like they were off to an embassy ball, long dresses, jewels, make-up, the most elaborate hair styles. You could have taken any of them to a royal garden party and they would have fitted straight in. In this heat too, I just couldn't work it out.

Then I spotted Desmond from the ship, he is one of the servers in the carvery and he has been on the QE2 since its maiden voyage so I asked him. He tried not to laugh but placed a reassuring arm around my shoulders and explained gently to me that they were really men dressed up as women offering their services. I studied them again with a jaundiced eye and I still couldn't see the join. Then this little girl tugged at my arm. Benevolently I bent down to see what she wanted whereupon this child produces a price list that included several services that I had never heard of in my life and some that I couldn't in my wildest imaginings have even contemplated. I somewhat abruptly turned her down whereupon she offers to fix me up with her brother instead: 'He very clean boy sah, you like him, only 11.' Ah well, perhaps Blackpool isn't all bad.

    I decided that I'd feel better back on the ship and hailed a taxi. Now, what is it about me and taxi drivers? In Australia I had the Farting Antipodean, and now in Malaysia I had the Belching Burmese. Seriously, he belched all the time, even when speaking: 'Where to sah…brr?' 'Sah is from England…brr?' 'You want to go to…brr, ship?' Who do I get next I ask myself? The Vomiting Venezuelan? The Crapping Columbian? And as to what the Welshman might be doing doesn't bear to think!

    It was the Singapore Swings Ball that night as Singapore was the next port of call. The problem was that I think I had promised to take Carol but I wasn't sure as when she is talking I usually get distracted by the hairs sprouting out of her and forget to listen. I had been avoiding her for two days but the problem was that I really needed a new library book and she is the librarian, I couldn't go on relying on Paula to lend me some of hers, I simply cannot read another Daphne De Maurier. So I put on me white suit from Hong Kong, the one that makes me look like a rubber planter, and strolled down to the library. Carol wasn't there, instead sitting in her place was this Chinese girl. Wow, she looked super, she was slim with that long, straight, black hair all down her back all wrapped up in a brilliant red kimono. It was only when she spoke that I realised it was Carol. It's all Daniella's fault, the cunning little cow, her and her weird sense of humour! Apparently, Carol went to her bemoaning the fact that I never took our relationship through to it's ultimate culmination and instead of recommending a razor Daniella told her that ever since Sootu I only fancied oriental girls. Still, we looked good together, me the rubber planter with his Chinese leisure girl. We were quite the thing on the dance floor, our Tango and Rumba are said to be so good they are obscene and it is true that when you have finished dancing the Tango with Carol your trousers are on back to front. And then we won the fancy dress prize. I didn't know whether to be pleased or insulted, I didn't even know there was a fancy dress competition taking place…I'll never be able to wear that white suit again.

30 Singapore

    I had a short note from the purser advising me not to take my knife ashore with me but I already knew this, it's a mandatory six month prison term for carrying a weapon of any description. Not a bad idea but then again I've been pleased to have it to hand some of the places I have visited on this cruise.

    Singapore's a nice place and it is amazing what this new bloke has done with it, now it's the most law-abiding city in the world. I can't make up my mind if it's worth it. To achieve all this it's virtually become a police state, you have to ask their permission to move house or stay out late that kind of thing, but then if you do you don't get stabbed on the way home. Apparently you get caned if you spit gum on the pavement…we can but hope!

I wandered around this big clean city where everybody is an automaton, you should see them cross the road, everybody waits at the crossings no matter how long they take to change, no one, and I do mean **no one** ever jay walks, not even the policemen of whom there are rather a lot. I visited the modern art gallery, it seems bigger than St Paul's and it is made entirely of glass…and it sparkles like it has just come out of the dishwasher. Now, what I want to know is who cleans it? I reckon they've got a whole colony of troglodytes armed with squee-gees who come out of the wood work when no one is looking. There were some good paintings but it was like looking at them in a hospital but the Hockney's fitted into that look and they have more of them than the Tate and the National combined.

I did some shopping and bought a new electric toothbrush, exactly the same one that had disappeared when Sootu left (I'm saying nothing) and it was a real bargain, only half as much again as it cost in Britain. Then it was off to The Raffles Hotel, you have to visit it, it's the law. I found it a bit sad because it is a truly magnificent relic from a time when Britain showed the rest of the world how to live. It is huge, bigger than a small town and so wonderfully old-fashioned with its Tiffin Room and Writer's Bar. Then I went and did what the guide book said I had to: I ordered a ***Singapore Sling***. Bloody hell fifteen pounds! And they are supposed to sell over 1000 a day. It was bright pink and frothy and tasted just like Benylin the cough medicine: I liked it. So I had another because it was harmless enough. Then I stood up and fell down again, and again, and again. Two waiters hurried forward and supported me under my arms and we did what is termed the **Sling Stagger** around the hotel...perhaps it wasn't quite as harmless as I had thought. The waiters deposited me in the Tiffin Room with an easy familiarity that smacked of constant practice and they gave me a huge newspaper to cover my face while I had a short nap. Two hours later a taxi driver called Ralph handed me over to the QE2 stewards and they supported me back to my cabin, this is becoming embarrassing...and I still don't really drink!

    I woke up at about 10 pm and hurried down to the Red Lion bar but I was in plenty of time. I had promised to take Mooweeelle to the St Patrick's day party and she hadn't arrived yet and then she did looking wonderful in these slinky velvet pants that made her hips look even better. It started off a good evening, my head had completely cleared after the **Slings and arrows of outrageous fortune** (sic) and Carol wasn't there so things were looking up. Then I went and opened my big mouth and told everybody I didn't like Guinness, never the wisest thing to do in a room full of Irishmen. Sam, the leader of the QE2 orchestra, decided it was his mission in life to teach me to like it and he never let up urging more and more people to buy me pints which even I couldn't refuse. It was about 12 when I climbed onto the tiny stage, switched on the karaoke unit and gave them: **Matchstalk Men and Matchstalk Cats And Dogs** followed by **Ernie The Fastest Milkman In The West!** And this, mind you, in front of about 100 professional musicians. Oh dear. Paula, who is honest in a kind of womanly way, said, 'It was a completely unorthodox rendition of an otherwise well loved couple of songs.' Mooweeelle, who is very nice, said, 'It was Tres Bon, and after all, ma petite, everybody understoods zat you had been, how we say it, drinking likes the camel.' Daniella, who I love dearly but who isn't nearly as nice, said, 'It was the most hideous sound I have ever heard since I crashed my mum's car into some corrugated iron railings.' And Dorcus, who is neither honest, nor very nice, said 'Nick, it was utter crap!'

    When I awoke the following lunchtime I went to the dance class and Warren, I'm sure at Daniella's suggestion, did the Paso Doble, the dance with all the stamping and shouting, it was just what my poor head needed. Afterwards I was walking with Daniella when we spotted Sam (the start of it all) sitting by himself in the Crystal Bar. He is dead easy to spot because he shaves his scalp twice a day and to be honest it really suits him because he has a perfectly shaped head like Yul. With Daniella's urging I crept up behind him and gave him a brisk slap around the back of his head, just like in Benny Hill. Ooo, I caught him beautifully, it was the perfect revenge to go with his perfectly shaped head. In fact everything only started to go a tad askew when he turned around to reveal he was someone I had never seen before. Apparently he was a brand new passenger who had just got on and was sitting in the bar while they made sure his cabin was ready. Of course, as this is my life we are talking about here, he had Sam's head and I came trolling along at exactly the right time. 'Oh dear,' thought I when he turned his unfamiliar face in my direction, a look of hurt bewilderment spread all over it, 'What we need here is a fast explanation followed by a profuse apology.' So I ran for it leaving Daniella to handle the embarrassing situation. She claimed later that she had told him that I was a relation of the Captain's and I was completely round the bend but quite harmless. Typical, you leave a woman a simple job to do and they turn it into a pig's breakfast!

31 Thailand

We arrived in Thailand. Feeling a bit jaded after all the drinking, dancing and head slapping, I stayed in bed until eleven so when I finally made it ashore to the motorbike rental shack nearly everything had already gone. All he had left was a nice staid little scooter and the most ridiculous Harley you have ever seen in your life. It was decorated in a piercing metallic blue that hurt your eyes and was so big that you couldn't stand it up on your own. But after Bali I think I've begun to learn my lesson, my shoulder still isn't right and lately I've started to realise that maybe it is worth staying alive a little longer. I bargained with the woman on the desk, or rather the kitchen table (it wasn't the poshest of places you understand). She asked for forty pounds but I beat her down to thirty, after all I only wanted it for a couple of hours. It was only after I was on my way that I ran through the maths in my head and realised that she had been asking for four pounds not forty! Oh, I did feel a worm, I gave her a ten pound tip when I got back. Anyway, the Harley went like a bird, it's almost like sitting on top of a big car, and it doesn't jump forward when you find which handle is the throttle, it sort of surges smoothly.

The bit of Thailand I saw was okay but it was a typical Far East country and if you were put down randomly in any of them you wouldn't be able to tell where you were, a bit like European countries I expect. On the whole it was alright but I didn't get arrested, I didn't fall off, I didn't even get drunk…I didn't even meet a farting taxi driver! I won't be going there again.

I went to a party early on the evening in The Mad Preacher's cabin. Fifteen of us in room the size of a shoebox and surprisingly it went quite well. The Mad Preacher is off my table and he's definitely odd, he's a vet now but he's an ex-ordained preacher and he has the staring eyes of a fanatic, I can see him burning me at the stake for my own good. Every day he throws a message in a bottle over the side, he's been doing this for over ten years and now has a network of loonies all over the world who keep in touch. Still he was a generous host and entertained us all with the souvenirs that he and his wife have purchased. Ooo, they have got some crap! You know the real terrible stuff you see in the very cheapest shops? And the way you think, who on earth would buy that monstrosity? Well, it's him! He's got an alarm clock in the shape of a mosque and when it goes off an Imam comes out and plods around the top calling the faithful to prayer. Then there's the huge snake made entirely of bottle tops, you brush past it and it rips holes in you. And there's a great plastic clampy sort of thing for holding your burger in and a fish the size of Moby that issues you a cigarette when you bend it's tail from side to side…oh, it's ghastly!

I'm nearly as normal as I've ever been (yes, yes, yes). Ever since we threw my Prozac off the back of the ship things have been improving. Paula says I am less aggressive now and I've stopped latching onto people and telling them my woes. And then I went to the Lido for lunch with Paula and Daniella and this grotty little steward snatched my tray off me and waved his hand in my face. Obviously the thing to do was to explain quietly that I wasn't jumping the queue and didn't want a meal I was just fetching my customary hunk of Brie and bunch of grapes. Things can always be settled by reasoned discussion, manners and a smile. So I grabbed him and had him bent backwards over the Bai Marie trying to force his head into the pea and ham soup (with Indian spices and garlic croutons) when gentle feminine hands persuaded me that I was perhaps going down a wrong path. Ooo, I was cross, the problem is when you are surrounded by women is that you can't hit anyone, and they are so understanding, it makes you sick! Then the Rottweiler arrived. Now the Rottweiler is the manageress of the Lido and she is this tall and very beautiful woman of about thirty but she is very tough, everyone is scared of her, even her husband. Immediately everybody relaxes, it's a bit like having Charles Bronson walk in the room. I'm still insisting that the grotty little steward comes with me to the gym where we will sort things out properly (oh dear, I can still hear myself saying it). The Rottweiler handles everything, she apologies sweetly to me then, and this I swear is true, she takes the steward by the scruff of his grotty neck and leads him away, presumably to walk the plank. The last thing I heard her saying was: 'It must be your fault, Dr Walker's a very nice man.' So, no arguments there then.

    I've got my sense of humour back and keep on getting invites to people's parties, actually they're a bit of a pain, they sort of muck up your routine. The bloke in the next cabin has made an official complaint about me and says that I keep on waking him up at night with my laughing and this mind you from someone who slams every door in sight and plays **Right Said Fred** at full blast every afternoon. We'll soon sort him out! I ordered him a huge breakfast of prunes and **All Bran** this morning and cancelled his seat in the dining room so he had to sit on his own by the toilets for evening dinner. I've put his name down for the tug-of-war team and he's lusting after Mary

(Big Ones) Boswell, the florist who is organising it so he won't dare back out. What he doesn't know is that most of the opposing team are from the crew who hate all the staff and passengers...there'll be some heads caved in there! I'm not finished with him yet, I just hope he puts some laundry out.

You know those people who are everywhere? Some people you don't see all week but you trip over others twenty times a day. Well, remember the chap whose head I slapped? He is of course, one of the latter. He's everywhere! We've never actually spoken, he just sits there gazing at me with this hurt expression on his face. If I'm in the bar he's there gazing at me across the rows of drinks. In the restaurant, he's sitting at a table right across the room but by a freak of seating every time I look up I can see him through a gap in the diners, it's putting me off my food. Talking of the restaurant, my waiter, Shakkir, has adopted me. He no longer gives me the menu to study just brings me what he thinks I'll like. Last week I tried to get turkey but he brought me veal instead, 'You wouldn't have liked that turkey, Dr Walker.' Once a week, on a Thursday, he insists I have a complete change from my normal round of beef and fish and he brings me all different dishes that aren't even on the menu. One evening I had nine courses and three of them were sweets and I ended up with a cappuccino coffee. Nothing I do can dissuade him from these actions and my dinner companions find the whole thing hilarious. Funnily enough, I find I enjoy the meal best on those nights.

It's India next and I've booked to go to the Taj Mahal. I wasn't going to because it is a three day trip and costs 5000 pounds but Daniella, who has been everywhere but the Taj Mahal, said that it was her dream so I had to go so I can gloat. I was summoned to the pre Taj meeting with the most curt note so having a bit of a seethe I went along. The note issuer stood up and after talking about himself for ten minutes gave us this vital advice: we would all need film for our cameras, we would all need batteries for our cameras and it would be hot so we must all drink plenty of water. He then repeated this three times so I stood up and asked whether we should all wear clean underwear…this got a round of applause but he was so thick-skinned (or thick) that he didn't get it. He then supplied us with the ship's itinerary for the visit which we had all been issued when we booked the cruise weeks ago. Next he proceeded to read it in a very slow patronising way so I stood up again and asked for a show of hands for everyone who could read. As this seemed to be everybody in the room, by unanimous consent, we all abandoned the meeting and left him to himself.

32 India

The Taj Mahal is the most testing tour on the world cruise. This is the itinerary: we leave the ship at 11 and board the bus for Colombo airport. There is a two-hour wait before a two hour flight to Madras then another two-hour wait before a two-hour flight to Delhi. The drive to the Palace Hotel is a welcome change to the pattern, it only takes 90 minutes. The following morning is a seven am start followed by a four hour drive over the most incredible roads to Accra. On arrival there is a visit to some kind of fort then the Taj that same afternoon. There is a banquet on the evening then it is up at five am for the traditional dawn visit to the Taj. Then it is another four-hour drive back to Delhi for some sightseeing before another two-hour wait at the airport for the flight back to Mumbai. After that it is a snap, all that is left is an hour's sightseeing tour and a drive back to the ship. But it didn't quite work out that way!

    The early lunch on board the ship was beef and chips, very ordinary for the QE2, but delicious. My cheering section came to lunch with me and Daniella, the bitch, brought Carol with her. When it was time to say goodbye they all watched and applauded as Carol gave me a lingering kiss, it was like kissing Desperate Dan. Daniella gave a heart wrenching aah as the hairy one said she'd miss me…I'm going to have to do something about her.

    If you've never spent a long wait in an Indian airport then it's an experience I urge you to miss. As the scheduled two hours stretched to five I pushed open the door of a tatty room and unwired the electric socket so I could connect up my computer. I was sitting cross legged on the dirty floor working away when a be suited little Indian came and jabbered at me. Me? A passenger on the QE2! I told him to bugger off and do something useful like fetch me a cup of coffee…he did too. The flight when it came was less than luxurious, except for those who had upgraded to first class, it was rated an internal flight (obviously) so they don't have to give you as much space as a continental flight. I was sat next to a Japanese student with ADHD and he simply would not keep still, even when he read a paper he managed to spread it across the front of all three seats in his row. Then he starts unpacking his bag and opening various purchases he had evidently made, you know, like mystical computer equipment and unidentifiable bits of electrical gear. I sat there crushed up into a tiny space with the vibrating Jap next to me and wondered just on what I was spending five thousand pounds. Finally my seat mate opened a yogurt so expansively that it splattered all over me, the seats in front, and the obnoxious kid sitting behind me kicking my seat. I leaned over real close to Bruce Lee and gave him a little bit of guidance and advice then I further looked to his well being by confiscating his food tray and telling the stewardess that he had decided not to eat. The rest of the journey was spent in a frozen silence.

    The flight to Delhi was only delayed by two hours so that was a pleasant surprise and the coach was waiting for us when we arrived. To be fair, everything that Cunard had control over was fine, but I guess no one is ever going to be able to hold the airlines accountable, they can get away with anything just by murmuring the words: passenger safety. Both the hotels we stayed in were five star so the annoying upgraders weren't able to make us feel inadequate.

    None of my particular friends were on the trip and that was okay, I was able to retreat into my own world without the annoyance of having to make idle chatter with anybody (miserable git). My iron rule when travelling is not to eat and to carry my own water and this I felt was particularly important in India, what with my dodgy stomach it simply was not wise to risk it. Anyway, my constitution could well do with break from all the food. I went to the hotel shop and bought some packets of biscuits and crisps and had a wonderful evening meal lying on my bed and watching *Cagney and Lacey* on Indian television. Then about eleven I felt like a stroll and wandered downstairs. I loved the comment from the receptionist when I asked him if it was safe to walk around late at night: 'Don't go to the right sir, and walk in the middle of the road.'

The following morning the coach was waiting for us at seven, unfortunately the upgraders kept us all waiting for another hour. Bobby, the organiser (a nice bloke) was very polite to them, sadly I wasn't quite as polite. After a quick consultation they elected to move to another coach and then looked somewhat peeved when this elicited a spontaneous round of applause from the other passengers.

The coach was wonderful, small because of the roads, but first class. Cunard books twice as many coaches as needed so we can all have a double seat to ourselves and there was an Indian steward with a ice box full of drinks to see to our every need. The roads were not quite as first class. They were indescribable, but I'll have a go anyway. Imagine the roads you see in the movies of Germany invading Russia during the second world war, then further imagine they had just been strafed by a squadron of tank buster planes and baked solid by a blistering sun. Then scatter stones the size of something Geoff Capes tosses around and cram them full with every type of disreputable vehicle you can think of…it still won't be enough, you have to add thousand and thousands of pedestrians all plodding gamely towards the city. Some incredible number of people like 10,000 a day give up their homes in the countryside and invade the city in search of a better life. If you haven't been to Indian then you don't know what poverty is!

But hey, we're from the QE2, we are tourists so we've got the bell! Another Indian is employed to stand leaning out of the window ringing the side bell furiously because it has been ordained that tourists have right of way. Ambulances, old ladies, children in prams, even policemen leap out of the way when they hear the sound of the tourist bus coming. So we hurtled through the crowds at breakneck speed but the problem was that even though we have the ultra modern, exceptionally well sprung coach, it still has to deal with the roads. I was once on a course in Scotland where this mad SAS major was teaching us all how to really drive a 4 by 4. On the last day he took us down a wildly rushing river at about 50 miles an hour and over the side of a cliff, our bus driver would have laughed at that, to him it would have been like driving a golf cart around St Andrews. I admired the driver, he looked about 12, but he had a wonderful vitriolic disposition. He spent nearly all the journey, one foot on the accelerator, one hand on the wheel, and the rest of his body out of the side window hurling abuse at other drivers. The bit I liked best though was on leaving Madras. We were leading the other two coaches, we weren't supposed to but he had overtaken the other two down a side street that didn't look like it could handle two bicycles going in different directions. We were steaming along, quite happily, when we come to a side road where two policemen were setting up a barrier of orange cones. The driver stiffened when he saw them and making an instantaneous decision he wrenches the wheel around and with an eldritch scream of tyres we take the side road on two wheels. The other two drivers, not to be outdone, also manage to get around with no more than a small loss of paintwork and the full breakfast of one of the upgraders.

Our driver powers forward aiming for the policemen who leap for their lives, the one my side falling face forwards into the ditch, I never did find out what happened to the other. Our driver howled abuse at the scuttling guardians of the law and we rocketed off down the road scattering orange cones in our wake.

I never could work out quite what he had against policemen or maybe it was traffic cones, I mean, we weren't even going down the bloody side street in the first place.

33 The Taj Mahal

So, I've joined that elite group of human beings who have seen the Taj Mahal. Was it worth it? Well, I wouldn't do it again, it is just too inaccessible but it's nice to have something to boast about (especially in front of Daniella). It is impressive, beautiful, peaceful, it is as good as you imagined, but perhaps not quite as big. The inside is nothing, the other buildings not worth the trouble, but the outside is everything. It was even better by dawn's early light and the birds singing gave it an almost religious feel. All in all, a pretty nifty tomb!

We were searched at the door for any objects that could do damage, then searched twice more. I had to leave my knife at the door and was feeling slightly embarrassed about it but when I saw what weaponry the other visitors left behind my knife paled in comparison. For the rest of my time in India I was looking at everybody wondering if they were the ones carrying four foot machetes down the legs of their trousers. There were guides everywhere but everything was right there for you to see so we all just wandered about. The group of Indians I admired most made a living by showing rich idiots the best spots from where to take photographs, truly. You'd have to be a perfect idiot to need their services but the world is full of perfect idiots because there were hoards of them at it.

There is a big pressure group inside India that is attempting to get the Taj recognised as one of the wonders of the world. At first you agree with them but when you have looked more closely you understand why it isn't. The whole thing is off centre because it is the tomb of an Emperor (Mughal Emperor Shah Jahan) and his Empress (Mumtaz Mahal) but he had to be put in the centre because, hey, he's the boss. So room had to be made off to one side of him for his Empress and he originally built it for her…dickhead! Then there's the carvings, from a distance they look wonderful but close up they are rudimentary and crude indeed. Still, taken as a whole, the place is still incredible.

I wandered away from the main party. I've developed a reputation for this, all the tour guides have been warned just to supply me with the time the bus leaves and then to forget about me. There was a mosque to the side and bugger me if two blokes didn't try the same scam as in Jamaica. Only this time they didn't have knives as we had all been through the same security. I had taken my shoes off and immediately I had been greeted by a little Indian man who led me through a very narrow door into a dark room. I ducked through it and knew I was in trouble. Another, taller man, carrying a walking stick, moved across and blocked my way out again. This time I wasn't in the tiniest bit amused! I was very tired from the journey and somehow being threatened in a mosque and at the Taj Mahal made it one hundred times worse. And even worse than that, both these guys must have been over sixty. Do I look like an easy mark?

I put on my cross look (you make the bottom of your eyes go all flat and show your bottom teeth, I used to practise in the mirror) and I slapped the side of the tall one's head with my foot (remember I was in stockinged feet). Then I grabbed the other one by his white shirt collar and did my controlled punch that just dented his nose by a millimetre and my uncontrolled karate roar that dented his eardrums by considerably more. They both looked shaken and I introduced myself as a karate instructor…a very cross karate instructor! They became very subdued and I'm not surprised for they weren't exactly tough guys. I told them in a very quiet voice that I was going to return to my group now and if any one of them had been at all bothered then I was coming back and I was going to be even crosser. It's a damn shame. Everywhere you go.

The hotel was incredible. My room was huge and luxurious, the bed so large that I was glad to be alone, I'd have never found Sootu in there. I went for a swim in the pool, glad to get a bit of exercise, then I changed into my shorts and went and had a brandy in the bar. Swipe me, fifty two pounds! And I don't really like brandy, I just thought ordering a coke looked a bit pathetic. Then the barman leans conspiratorially over the bar and advises me that they did not encourage the wearing of shorts in the bar. I said, quote: 'For fifty bleeding pounds I'll come in here just wearing a condom if I feel like it.' He nodded philosophically, I've said before, the staff in these five star places are trained not to argue. Still, I actually agreed with him, it was just so hot, so I took my drink outside and lay on a sun lounger in the air- conditioned covered patio.

Included in the trip was: ***A Journey Through Indian Cuisine*** and this was the excuse to serve Indian food of questionable quality at every possible chance. The rest of the party had gone mad and had stuffed themselves with cold buffets, hot buffets, fresh seafood, hot curries, very hot curries and real bum-burning curries. But tonight it was the highlight of the food trip, there was to be a seven-course traditional Indian meal served on the old-fashioned silver platters. I had taken some stick already on the trip because I had stuck to my packets of biscuits and crisps but tonight every member of the party took the opportunity to taunt me as they staggered out of the dining room still gasping for breath. Everybody, it appeared, was very sorry for me missing the experience of my life. Their experience had just begun!

I went to bed early and had a peaceful night's sleep. None of them were to have any sleep at all but they certainly got plenty of exercise! When I woke at five for the traditional dawn visit to the Taj I nearly went back to bed but I was so glad I didn't. Surprisingly there was almost no one for the coach and I went with Bobby, the coach driver and a couple of assorted women. You get there just as the sun is showing over the horizon and it backlights the Taj and now you realise that it really is pink. It sort of glows and just as the sun's rays hit you the birds start to sing. The Taj building is just how you've seen it in the photographs but it is best viewed from a distance over the pools and gardens. We didn't even bother to go inside, a small group of about thirty of us just stood and watched as the sun climbed quickly up the sky and turned the flamingo pink into a sort of faded elegant white.

We drove back to the hotel for breakfast and I had a welcome cup of coffee with some of my biscuits then I went and sat outside waiting for the rest of my party. They were late, but this time it wasn't just the upgraders but everybody. Bobby disappeared upstairs to hurry them up and at last they came out blinking into the sunlight looking like they had just come last in the Iron Man triathlon…which I suppose in some ways they had.

Pale and wan, clutching feebly at marauding stomachs, they limped down to the coach for the four-hour drive back over those incredible roads. But it was to take much longer because Indian coaches don't have toilets. Nor does India have public conveniences. A half way comfort stop had been included at this posh restaurant but this was much too far away for the majority of them. Cries of: ***stop the bus! Stop the bus!*** rent the air every few miles and there would be a frantic scrabble for the door and a desperate search for the nearest bush. Guess what? India doesn't have bushes either! All dignity perished in the basic needs of humanity. Was it just my wishful thinking or did the upgraders seem to be suffering more? As one particularly irritating man stumbled past on his urgent mission I grabbed hold of his sleeve to make him tarry a while. I pointed: 'There's an executive class patch of dirt over there,' I said. But he didn't seem to be in the mood for humour, just groaned and staggered away.

Well, I'll stop gloating now. As the one lady said to me, when she could speak again, 'If you had just once said, *I told you so!* We could have all set on you and killed you and anybody else who tried to stop us. It would have helped!'

34 Mumbai

The coach took us to Delhi to wait for our flight. We did some sightseeing and India is truly an amazing place. Only a hardy few of the party remained on the coach for the drive around the others retreated to a hotel to rent a room (or should I say a toilet?) for the few hours we had free.

I wandered around with the remnants and just as you see in the movies there were snake charmers and bear baiters and tiger...well, whatever it is you do to a tiger. I stood gazing down this shopping street in the distance and I could not for the life of me work out what I was seeing: it looked like the finely milled grain shot from a shotgun cartridge all rolling about. Then it suddenly came into focus and you wonder why you didn't see it before. Those black beads were the heads of thousands of people. That's the thing about India, there are a lot of people about, still, they have to put 1000 million people somewhere. Poverty is everywhere but you can't do anything about it, I tried giving this girl of about fourteen with a crippled baby a dollar and almost immediately a hoard of beggars descended on us all shouting their heads off. We retreated to the coach and barricaded the door but it didn't put them off they surrounded the coach banging on the windows and rocking the coach from side to side. It really was quite hairy but then a column of immaculate policemen arrived from out of nowhere and set about the mob with canes. You wouldn't believe it, they just carved a way through the hoard slashing at bottoms and legs like a public school headmaster. The head policeman came aboard and explained in very good English that we really mustn't give money to the poor as this will always happen.

But, there's wealth everywhere as well. Which country in the world has the most millionaires? America? Japan? Germany? No, amazingly it's India! Our Indian guide explained it to us: India has one of the worst ratios of poor to rich people in the world, only 4.5% are said to be rich but in a country of one thousand million people that means there are forty-five million very rich people indeed. That's not far off half the number of English in the whole world.

India hadn't finished with us yet. We took the flight to Mumbai (what we used to call Bombay) and it was getting dark when we landed. We were supposed to have a guided coach tour through Mumbai and on to meet the ship at ten. But the upgraders hadn't finished being a pain in the arse just yet. One of the women insisted on visiting a hospital and we had to sit in the coach waiting for her, after two hours and a fortune in medical fees the doctor took one look at her and told her to drink plenty of water. My suggestion of leaving her in India was generally welcomed by the passengers but the guides thought it would be politically insensitive to return to the QE2 one short. So we waited, and waited and waited. She was finally released at about quarter to ten so it was agreed that we must make a dash for the ship as it was scheduled to leave at eleven.

There were three coaches we could choose from, well, more two for everybody else because all the upgraders had to wait for me to be seated before they could get on another coach. Well, coaches one and three went straight to the pier but guess who had chosen the coach which had the Indian tour guide who had been rehearsing his speech for three months and was going to deliver it come hell or high water? I was so glad, it was a trip that will linger in my memory forever!

We would drive around for a time with the Indian expatiating all the wonders of Mumbai then Bobby would come hurrying up the aisle and there would be a lot of furtive whispering: 'Straight back to the bloody pier, right! If we're late the ship will go without us!' 'Oh yes sir. Straight to the pier sir. I understand sir.' The guide and the driver would swap terse comments then the ship would appear off to our right and Bobby would relax, then the driver would abruptly swerve off down a side street and the guide's spiel would start up again. Bobby would come hurtling up the aisle and the guide would try to dodge past him (not an easy thing to do in the gangway of a coach) all the while still shouting at the top of his voice: 'These are the colleges of education…oh, yes sir, I understand sir, the pier sir…you will notice the Colonial style of the buildings, that's because it was the headquarters of the British Raj…oh, the pier is just down here sir…this is a shortcut, it takes us right past Mumbai's central square…pardon sir…oh yes, the central square is right near the quay sir and here you can see Mumbai's main laundry district, it is so cheap even the poorest of the people can have clean clothes…pardon sir…oh yes, it's particularly close to the quay so…so, they could get the water for the washing.'

Everyone was so serious because they all thought the ship would leave without us except for me who was hysterical. It was the best coach journey I have ever had in my whole life, it was like being kidnapped by Alan Whicker! We reached the ship's tender two hours after everybody else and as were clambering aboard you could still hear the guide's voice bellowing away in the background: 'All this area was reclaimed from the sea as late as 1957...'

The ship waited for us, of course it did! It was their tour and their responsibility so they were hardly likely to abandon fifty odd of their most wealthy passengers to the auspices of India! But, the bonus came with the upgraders, because the only place they could wait, away from the beggars, was in the tender itself, and the water was very rough. They had been gradually recovering from their experiences with the Delhi Belly and now sea sickness started affecting them at the other end…you simply cannot imagine people have that much food inside them!

35 Dubai

I got up early in Dubai. I had arranged to meet Carol at eleven and I wanted to make absolutely sure I missed her. She is very worried about me, she believes that my total inability to remember appointments with her is a syndrome left over from my breakdown. She says I should go to aromatherapy but I said I'd already been and told her about the farting taxi driver in Australia.

I slunk past the library and crept ashore and the minute I was safe I leaped into a taxi and we made for the hills. Dubai is so rich it is obscene. You wonder where all that money for the oil goes to, well it's Dubai! Everything is so new that it makes you realise just how old Britain is…and how much you miss it. The Burj Al Arab hotel is here, that's the one that is built to look like a sail and claims to be seven star, the prices certainly are: the cheapest room costs over $1000 and the dearest comes in at $28,000, that's per night! I find that sort of thing obscene but that's where I was heading for I had been despatched by the crew on a secret mission. There's a tango room and everybody wanted to go and see the show (apparently you can join in) and it is danced every single night of the year. Except, of course, for Mohammed's birthday…guess which day it was! But it meant I had the chance of looking around the hotel. I flashed my QE2 card at the security guard and fortunately he couldn't read but still stood in my way and asked to see my room key. But I'm hardened to these people now and I put on my snottiest look and waved him out of my life and strode magnificently into the reception…the hotel is purported to be the most expensive in the world so anybody visiting it is super rich and not to be trifled with. And it is amazing in there, the space is breathtaking and there are pools just everywhere and beautiful bars and restaurants and shops. Not that you need to buy any food because there are small, but very posh, buffets all around, you just help yourself to anything. Then I realised that I was being tracked by a security man so I put on my look and walked straight at him and he jumped out of my way and I headed imperiously off down one of the corridors. I think I would have got away with it too if I hadn't boldly flung open a door and marched inside only to find it was an electricity cupboard. He didn't really believe in me after that and my QE2 card, for the first time, had no effect. He was quite nice about it and he escorted me to the door. Another guard joined him and had the effrontery to put his hand on my arm until I advised him seriously not to do this.

   The bloody sultan of Dubai (the small -s is intentional) came on board to greet the passengers. The fat turd turned up two hours late and most of the brain dead passengers cheered him when he finally condescended to arrive. He wandered through them tossing gold bracelets as he went and all these rich, arrogant passengers were scrambling to catch them, he loved it. I dunno, we take some tent dwelling brigand, discover oil in some unusable bit of desert that he just happens to be grazing his camel on at the time, build a refinery and then hand the whole lot over to him Scott free. Then he proceeds to make himself a billionaire by blackmailing us! Send a gunboat I say.

With my liberal sentiments I thought it advisable to avoid his visit and elected to retire to my cabin. Now, the only way back to my cabin that doesn't involve passing the library is to go through the Queen's Ballroom where Colin (yet another cruise director) is keeping the idiots amused while they waited on the sultan's pleasure.

'Nick,' he cried spying me, 'aren't you waiting to see the sultan of Dubai?'

'If I had wanted to see a fat, undereducated crook,' said I, 'I would have dropped in to see Ronnie Cray before he died.' There was a very loud silence which was shattered by furious applause from the Mad Preacher from my table.

'Aren't we talking about a sand nigger here Nick?' he howled. Cries of 'Shame,' rent the air alongside mutterings of support. Nick, always ready to back a colleague, hurried off to his cabin. The Mad Preacher wasn't at dinner tonight, I think he my have been stoned (to death that is). Colin came over to me that night and said if there was ever anything I really wanted to be sure and to ask him first. Wasn't that nice of him?

It was another captain's party the same night so I went to the casino instead. It was awful, gambling in these places has become so structured that you might as well just hand you money over at the door and cut out the middle man. Poker was just a procession of money going one way so I had a go at roulette and tried a doubling up system. It was okay, at least I got to play for a couple of hours but he main attraction was the other loonies at the table. One bloke kept putting hundred dollar chips on the single numbers, he lost over ten thousand dollars while I was losing just fifty. When he finally wandered off the croupier told me that he did the same every single night, I wondered whether he was related to the sultan.

    Paula came and found me. Apparently the Captain's party had been full of interest. Carol went, not surprisingly because I had agreed to meet her there, and Mooweeelle went, which was more surprising because I hadn't. Anyway, Daniella, of course, deliberately introduced them. I need to explain that this is one of the poshest parties on the whole cruise and everybody goes including the sultan and one of his wives. So, these two members of the QE2's staff start discussing me in virulent hissing whispers that get louder and louder. Everybody, so Paula says, was craning forward to hear the latest insult when Mooweeelle, who is a bit excitable, empties her glass of champagne into Carol's face, and several assorted bystanders who just happened to be standing too close. Well, Carol is educated and sophisticated (in spite of the hair) and talks with a middle class accent but she still hails from the East End and she immediately unleashes a punch that takes Anthony (the party host), who was trying desperately to intervene, full in the left eye. The Mad Preacher, who had reappeared unscathed, gives his furious applause again and howls: 'Woo, nice one Tyson.' And the sultan, who has strolled over to see what all the fuss is about turns to the Captain and says, 'A strange name for a girl, Tyson?'

Anyway, both of the girls are up for a Master's warning, which is serious because three of those and you are off the ship. Strangely neither of them seem to want to discuss the incident with me!

36 Oman

I knew all about Oman already. I had met an Argentinean girl at Dava Sobel's lecture the week before. She had told me that of all the places she had travelled then Oman was the most beautiful and she had lovely eyes so she must be right. So, I went and it was nasty. To be fair it was just the one little town but maybe that's the high spot of Oman, for all I know people may travel hundreds of miles just to visit it. It looked just like Tipton built inside a quarry…that's it exactly: Tipton built inside a quarry! They rattle on about how the traditional town (Tipton) cannot expand because of its rocky surroundings (the quarry). I shouldn't think anyone would want to expand it, I don't imagine even Stevie Wonder would like the way it looks.

  Anyway, they had already pissed us all off. Suddenly, for no reason, they had stuck an entry fee on all Americans so our whole American contingent stayed aboard. I would have liked to stay with them to show solidarity but I had a vital mission to accomplish. I was running short of the one necessity that was absolutely vital to my sanity, the big question was: could Oman supply this essential commodity? Well, in the space of half an hour I was offered: heterosexual and homosexual sex, oral and anal sex, a pretty girl who I could flog or who would be delighted to flog me, marijuana, crack cocaine and heroin, any kind of alcohol I could name in this dry country, stolen watches, cigarettes and amazingly a camel…but nowhere was there a piece of chewing gum to be found. I only have four sticks left and four days at sea, I may have to go back on Prozac.

  I was back on board for elevenses and I will ever be eternally grateful that this was so because otherwise I would have risked missing one of the funniest spectacles on the entire cruise. Two old men had a fight on the boat deck! They had fallen out over whose deck chair it was and as their combined age was more than 180 it was a sight worth seeing. Each had a walking stick and each really needed it so the hilarious thing was that every time they used it to swipe at one another they would sag off to one side as their knees collapsed. In the end they had to come to a gentleman's agreement and one of them held onto the deck rail while the other kept hold of the helicopter deck stairs. The problem they had is that the QE2 is a very big ship so even at full stretch with their sticks they still couldn't quite reach one another so had to be content to hurl abuse in the gaps between strolling couples. I lay on the deck helpless with laughter until security arrived and led them gently away for a glass of warm milk…shame!

    I went to the charity dance, this is when you buy tickets to dance with members of the staff and entertainment groups. There were ten women down one side of the dance floor and ten men down the other side and you paid $10 for a dance all of which went to charity. I was thinking about this when it suddenly occurred to me that none of the men on board were going to buy a ticket for a dance, most would buy one not to dance. Cunard employs around 15 men dancers to act as partners for the single women…or the ones whose husbands won't dance. I fancied this as an idea to get a free cruise, because that's how they are paid, they don't actually get any money. That was until I had a word with one of them who was hiding behind the large curtains in the ballroom getting his breath back. He told me it was an absolute killer and most of them would only do two weeks at a maximum. They have to dance every single night of the cruise for three hours, then every morning we aren't in port they have to be there for the ballroom dance lesson and that's before the afternoon session in the disco downstairs. I became interested in them after that and watched them all one evening and realised that some of them have a little scam going. They are supposed to dance with every available woman but some get chosen much more frequently than others and then I spotted it, some of the old and very rich women, slip a $10 bill into their top packets after every dance…good money!

And now I was going to do it the other way, I was going to pay $10 to dance with women I didn't know. I nipped down and bought tickets for all 20 dances that night, yes, $200! That's 2 dances with each of the women and two of them were Daniella and Carol who I dance with anyway. Not another ticket was sold to a single man, the women bought hundreds. It's got to be said though that I was extremely popular if extremely knackered. Every dancer (except for Carol) was a professional, mostly from the theatre group on board, bloody hell, you only had to twitch your arm to indicate an underarm turn and off they went like a Catherine Wheel. Or you could try signalling a promenade to Daniella (who after all is the ex-world champion) and she takes off like Linford Christie in a skinhead bar. I had to have my whole dinner outfit dry cleaned again.

The following night didn't work nearly as well. I had managed to dodge both Carol and Mooweeelle and had finally achieved my long standing ambition of getting Yoshica onto the dance floor. Now Yoshica is Japanese like Sootu but older and more sophisticated. She is very attractive and elegant but as nervous as a bird. I have been trying to get a dance with her since Kobe. Well, let us be entirely honest: I really wanted to check out whether my theory about Japanese women bowing just before they…er, well, cement their affections with you. The problem was that Yoshica never dances just stands there wistfully swaying to the music so I had it all planned, I even had a waltz arranged with John (the announcer) to play at my signal. So finally I get her onto the floor and we Waltz around the room with me being so kind and showing her every move. When the music fades and we are left gazing romantically into each others eyes I murmur, 'Stay on, it's the Rumba next.' She screws up her face like she had just swallowed a bee and shouts, "No! No!' and rushes from the floor like a rat up a drain pipe. Then, get this, she goes off with this horrible little Frenchmen with a nasty little beard. The sympathetic bandsmen were all delighted, some of them were so delighted that they could hardly hold onto their instruments for the next song. And, as for Paula and Daniella, who had come along to witness my endeavours, they virtually had to go and change their underwear.

    News travels fast on this ship because when I went down to the Lido for my morning coffee I approached Dustin and she shouted out: 'No! No!' and hurried away…I'm going to have to do something about Daniella.

37 Petra

There's a man on board called Clement Nathaniel Eagleburger II. He's a postman, I assume you can guess his identity. Then there's a Jap on board who's called Hi Li, he's the managing director of a car firm. The world's gone mad, where's the justice in one man having 29 syllables to his name while some other poor sod has to make do with 4? I, of course, am very discrete about the whole thing, I merely address them by their full name at every opportunity: 'Will you pass the salt please Clement Nathaniel Eagleburger II?' and he never seems to appreciate it. Then there's: 'Hi, Hi Li, are you going for a Li down? I should warn you that the temperature is very Hi on deck and I do not Li, Hi Li.' They've got very little sense of humour these Japs.

John and June came and found me to ask if I would go with them to Petra. I wasn't keen, I'd been having a stomach upset for a couple of days and wasn't feeling that well, I'd blame the food at Oman but I didn't eat anything. Anyway, I finally agreed. The cruise trip was $180 plus $25 entrance and there were 18 coaches from the QE2 including 4 for the crew alone. It's a three-hour journey across the desert and there are lurid tales of gangs of rebels (rebelling against what? More sand?) kidnapping hostages. Only three people went on their own, guess which three? John and June said they would prefer to put their trust in **Super Nick.** Well, okay, I added the super. We arranged a deal with this taxi driver, me acting all menacing and John haggling away at the price until the poor man was completely intimidated. It was a super journey, sitting in an air-conditioned cab travelling through some memorable scenery. As for rebels, I've felt more threatened in Chelmsford, the road was as busy as the M6, any aspiring rebel would have been squashed flatter than a hedgehog if they had attempted to stop us.

Petra, the rose pink city, is another one of those places you visit once. It's a large village carved out of rock and only accessible through a narrow slit in the rock. Bloody hell, there's some walking involved, you are offered these donkeys if you can't manage the walk but you'd have to be one of those mad rodeo riders to try it. These donkeys hurtle around the place with their Arab drivers frantically hanging onto them for grim life. Only one of the crew tried it and he shot past us at about fifty miles an hour, both hands clasping frantically to the saddle while he raced alongside his feet moving in a blur. It was his rather pathetic, 'Oh, please, no faster,' as he whizzed by that got me going. We walked. You come to this great slit in the rock and sort of slide through, well, it feels like you have to slide but it's not really that narrow. Then you are in the city. It doesn't look rose pink to me, it looks like the colour of the sandy rock it is carved out of! When it comes down to it it's a scrabbly, collection of abandoned huts set in a scrap of desert. I wandered off and tried to inhale the atmosphere but I couldn't see it, if Petra was across the road to where I used to live in England I don't suppose I'd visit it more than once.

The organised trips had included a two-hour posh lunch (that's something everyone needs on the QE2, a posh lunch) but we took a picnic from my little friend in the Lido and we sat and ate it in one of the huts. Then we had a long camel ride and John had an even longer argument with the camel drivers. June and I sat peacefully as first of all the police got involved, then the other camel drivers and finally the personnel of at least two other trips. I found it hilarious, June found it boring, she says he always has an argument wherever he goes. Finally things were sorted out and John got $1 a head knocked off. It's the principle, John maintains, and I am prepared to believe him because he is a millionaire. Finally, when we could think of nothing else to do, we started to make our way back along the long walk. I was feeling less and less well, my head felt like I wasn't fully in it and then all at once I sort of sunk to the ground. John and June had to haul me to my feet and support me for the last mile. June was delighted and kept introducing me to everybody we past: 'Hi, this is Nick our minder.' John was a little more brusque: 'Fine bleeding bodyguard you turned out to be!'

Finally they got me back to the taxi and I slept most of the way home. We started at 8 o clock and got back at 3 in the afternoon. The organised trips started at 6.45 am and they got back at 7 pm...all this for only $205 plus lunch and another $25 for tips for the drivers and guides. Guess what we paid (or rather John paid) $52 each. Oh brother are we hated throughout the ship!

What's going on? I've been dumped again! This time by Mooweeelle, the French bitch. The cheek of these women not letting me get in first. She caught me having a private lesson of Charleston from Summer (I know but she's in the theatre thingy) in the space invaders room. This doesn't refer to a room that is occupied by people who have invaded us from space but to the room where all the video game machines are, it is the one place on board where you can get privacy as there are virtually no kids on the cruise.

    Anyway, Mooweeelle came storming in, enrobed me in a positive deluge of shouted French of which the one phrase I could extricate with any confidence was the rather unusual one of: ***big stinky fart!*** An expression I hadn't come across before. Now the question is this, how did she know where to find me? And the other one is, how come Daniella just happened to be walking past like she is whenever anything happens to me? I have my suspicions! These were added to when I walked through the Red Lion later in the day where Daniella was innocently talking with a bevy of other staff and I distinctly heard the words Big Stinky Fart spoken in a false French accent.

38 Egypt

I was feeling better so I agreed to go with June and John to the Pyramids. I know the Pyramids quite well, the Poison Dwarf and I used to stop off in Cairo whenever we went SCUBA diving at Sharm El Sheik, but it's one of the places that always impresses me.

The ship arrived late at Suez and Cunard had cancelled the coach but had arranged for a whole fleet of taxis to take anybody who still wanted to go. We ignored the odious little Cunard rep who informed us that we had to use his taxis and instead took the shuttle bus into town. Eight other people, who had presumably learned their

lesson from the Petra trip, followed on behind…everyone putting their trust in Nick. I got hold of three taxis and John went into his protracted bargaining act, the rest of us sat drinking coffee while he bawled and shouted, but still, he's good at that bit. The Cunard rep had been asking $200 for a taxi and John finally agreed on $45 for as long as we wanted them. The odious little Cunard rep came slinking up and started telling the prospective passengers about crooked taxi drivers and violent robbers so I finished my coffee off and went and involved myself. I told the rep he was a Big Stinky Fart which made him blench and storm off in an offended manner. Then as the other passengers were still looking worried I took the drivers of the four taxis (one of them by the arm no less) over to the building that had a sign over it reading: **Tourist Police.**
There was this policeman sitting outside in the sun. He was so familiar that he was funny. He didn't look at all Egyptian but exactly like you think South American policemen look. He was fat and a captain and he was leaning right back in his chair with his polished booted feet up on a table. A long thin cigar dribbled smoke into the air and a long thin moustache dribbled down over his mouth. I asked him whether he would vouch for the four drivers and he catapulted forward and subjected them to a tirade of invective that I hadn't heard before since…since, well to be absolutely accurate, since the day before from Mooweeelle. The Captain then gave each of them a licence inspection followed by a car registration check, a finger in the face job and the laser stare treatment. He then turned to me and said casually: 'They be fine now,' and he returned to his siesta. The thing that really got to me during all this entertaining machinating was when he mimed wearing a pair of handcuffs to the drivers. It got to them too because

they were like lambs for the whole day. It took our driver an hour to stop shaking and thereafter I only had to say a word and he'd jump like a wasp had just stung his bum.

We returned to the huddle of passengers, who were now all looking suitably impressed, and John and June who both had proud smiles on their faces at their protégé performing so well…they looked exactly like the parents of a child genius who had just completed some intricate musical performance. I told the drivers we wanted fast and they cut the drive down from three hours each way to two. We got back in time for dinner, the Cunard lot didn't return until gone eleven. You know, I get the feeling at the next stop there will be a whole convoy of taxis following on behind us. We learned later that the others had all had an armed escort that had terrified them more than any group of terrorists.

I always like the Pyramids, the sheer scale of them never fails to impress. Most of the places you see abroad are a disappointment, either smaller or less glamorous than you have been led to believe, but the pyramids are bigger and there are more of them than you think. The thing I can never get over is that there is a primary school backing right onto them, it sort of blows me away that some kids actually mess about in the playground with the Pyramids hanging over them. Surprisingly John wasn't impressed. He had started of in life as an engineer and he was most disappointed, he said he could complete the whole lot in a couple of months given half a dozen JCBs and a good team of Irish navvies.

June and I sat on the sand while John marched off around them, I still wasn't feeling one hundred percent so I whimped out for once. June accepted a lucky stone off a camel driver when I wasn't looking and was then subjected to a demand for cash. I made him take it back and told him to bugger off whereupon he leaned forward over the head of his camel and told me in perfect, upper class English that I was a miserable git. I have been wondering ever since whether I finally had discovered Lord Lucan. Meanwhile John was having his customary row with another camel driver (I really don't know what he's got against them…it's always camel drivers!) so I wandered over and extricated him and when we got back June was surrounded by a positive barrage of beggars all trying to sell her bits of junk. Ah well, Egypt is Egypt. We packed up and made our way back again trailing the others in our wake.

On the following day we went through the Suez Canal. After the Panama Canal I was in no hurry to see it and I was right even the over-enthusiastic ones soon got bored. Basically it is a channel cut in the sand filled with water. Incredibly, it still costs 250,000 pounds to pass through it to gaze at another lot of sand!

I went to the gym and discussed with Maxine, the girl trainer, about shaving my head. The idea is to make myself look tough so I wouldn't automatically get mugged whenever I visited a third world country. It was mainly a joke but Maxine assured me that Carol cannot stand bald men and if I had it done then she'd never come near me again. Hmm, worth thinking about that one, but then again, Maxine is Daniella's friend so it might be a wind up…we'll have to see.

I am not going to see Pompeii. I am not! I am not! I am not! I know exactly what it'll be like: a load of uninteresting ruins with a swarm of Japanese taking pictures of bits of brick. I'm not going…and that's my final word on the matter.

39 Pompeii

So, I went to Pompeii. And guess what? It was a load of uninteresting ruins with a swarm of Japanese taking pictures of bits of brick. I swear, there was a cobbled road, just like they've got in Penzance, and there is this channel about six inches wide cut across it obviously for water…the bloody place was stiff with Japanese cameramen! They were all shoving and squeezing past one another to get a photo of this remarkable bit of brick. Don't these people have drains at home?

The day started well. I had breakfast with my cheering section because Dorcus is getting off at Pompeii, Paula and Daniella are staying on till New York. They told me that in their opinion I was fully cured and I thanked them for all their friendship and support and we all had a little cry. And, do you know what, I rather think I am cured, almost ready to return to real life in fact…I haven't fallen out with anybody for simply ages, even when a German refused to relinquish the gym bike I had booked all I did was smile chidingly and go off for a swim instead.

The day started to deteriorate from then on in. Carol caught me slinking past the library and asked me to come to see the show that she is presenting. She also told me that Pompeii is the best place to see on the whole trip and she would love to show me around on the afternoon so I rushed off and went in the morning instead. There's this kind of building, a bit like a London railway station, you have to go through to get ashore and right at the end is a newspaper kiosk. I was passing it when this little runt of an Italian came rushing out and asked for money. I was feeling in my pocket for a note when the bloody little turd grabbed my jacket, pushed me back up against the wall and told me to give him all I'd got. What is going on? He was only about five feet tall with a rat like skinny face. It was the insult, the sheer bloody cheek of it that really got to me. I grabbed him by the throat and the crotch and I was so angry I lifted him right off the floor and hurled him into a row of rubbish bins. He sort of collapsed over them and lay there amongst the overflow gurgling for breath. I was thinking of loosing a kick at a sensitive area or two but instead I managed to make myself walk away and stormed off into Italy looking for an argument. It wasn't going to be long.

  I found a taxi. It was at the head of a taxi rank and I climbed in and discussed for some time how much it was going to cost me to go to Pompeii and back again. After some argument we agreed on eighty pounds, I leaned on him and told him that would be eighty pounds in total including the tip and not to even try and ask for anymore. I also told him I was a policeman back in Britain so as to impress him more. Obviously he wasn't impressed by policemen, or anyway British policemen, because he drove me a mile to a deserted spot stopped the car and demanded more money. Oh, I was cross: everywhere you go people try and rip you off! The door to the taxi was locked so I wrenched the window down and opened it with the outside door handle. He immediately backed off and told me that eighty pounds would be okay but I completely lost it, I couldn't get his door open but his window was still down so he could try and placate me. I told him exactly what I thought of him, which wasn't good, then I said he shouldn't be a taxi driver he should be a refuse man and reached in and grabbed the car keys and tossed them in a skip full of stinking rubbish. He was absolutely stunned by this, he was literally speechless, so I helped myself to his taxi licence which was attached to the rear view mirror and marched off back down the road. The last I saw of him he was trying to climb up into the rubbish skip.

 I made it back to the taxi rank still fuming and told the little man in the police type box what I thought of them all and he was horrified. He tried to apologise and said action would be taken but I was too cross, I just demanded that he find me a taxi driver who would accept eighty pounds for the trip and he hurried to obey. The driver seemed a nice guy but I was still fed up with all Italians so I told him just to drive not talk so we went to Pompeii in absolute silence.

 I don't know what people like Carol see in these places, I don't have to describe Pompeii, you just have to watch ***The World at War*** when they show the devastation of Berlin and there you have it. I must be missing something, great parties of Germans stand around listening enthralled as a guide rambles on endlessly about bits of broken piping, and the Japanese, well, I've told you about the Japanese!

 I made it back to the ship, I was feeling a bit calmer by this time so I gave way and tipped the driver. He tried to apologise again about the other man but I didn't care I just wanted to get back to my insular life aboard.

 I decided to hide in the cinema in case I bumped into Carol but the movie was something about dog shows and a woman in front of me kept standing up and going through some sort of callisthenics so I decided to sneak out early. Not wishing to make a row I slid over the back of the seats not realising they were set on a raised dais. I fell to the floor with the most appalling crash and when I rose groaning to my feet the whole cinema was on their feet staring at me…I couldn't have made a more spectacular exit if I'd have been shot out of a cannon.

My cabin steward, remember him, Lito? Well, he's an excellent steward, friendly and happy and just respectful enough, and not too enthusiastic when he brings me my breakfast each morning. That is except when he gets a letter from home. You know when this happens because he is no stoic and even when he opens the door you know something is wrong, his face is to the floor and he speaks as if he is announcing the crack of doom. He has a wife and two children back in the Philippines, amazing though that seems because I'm sure he can't be much above ten…and he misses them very much. She writes to him every two weeks and I dread these days because it means that I have to go and sit with him in his cubby hole while he reads me the letter and has a good cry. It's amazing just how upset someone can get, I'm not belittleling his loneliness but, I mean, I once met a man who had under six months to live and he was a positive Chris Akabusi compared to Lito. It usually takes me an hour or more to get him up and moving in the real world again then he has to take me to the crew's storage to show me all the stuff he has bought for their home. You wouldn't believe it: TVs and washing machines and fridges! I mean you don't go on holiday and bring a bloody fridge back with you do you?

Anyway, the following morning was a Lito morning so I had an excuse for not meeting with Carol. She has become even more persistent since Mooweeelle dumped me, I really have to keep my hand on my holiday money when I escort her back to her cabin. Finally, I decided I must go and see her in the library…and, anyway, I had finished my library book. She was a bit thin-lipped about

Pompeii but in the end understood that I have a pathological fear of volcanoes that prevents me from going anywhere in the vicinity of one. But the upshot is that I have definitely agreed to go and see her show on the following evening…what's worrying me is the party afterwards!

40 Marseilles

Marseilles stunk of fish. It's understandable as it is a fishing port but it really stunk of fish! This is the town that The Union Corse (the French mafia) run but far from being exciting it is rather dreary. I wandered around for a while trying to find some excitement or glamour but all that happened was that the rain dripped steadily on me. I went into a coffee bar and had some French onion soup followed by a croque monsieur sandwich and some French fries. They were served with typical Gallic charm when the waiter virtually threw them at me and quite seriously I've had better onion soup in Chelmsford. The waiter then disappeared and no amount of shouting or thumping on the bar could raise him again and have you ever tried to eat chips without salt? Finally a local woman took pity on me and found some sachets of salt from her bag. This was virtually the only meal I tried to have ashore on the whole cruise and it only went to confirming me in my decision, though to be completely honest the service anywhere is going to be difficult to get used to after the QE2.

When I got outside again the sun had staggered out cheering the place up considerably and with it had come hoards of woman all dressed up in summer clothes. I sat in the park watching them. It's a surprising thing, but as my mother warned me years ago, French woman aren't very pretty…indeed they are not! If you want proof then try watching The Tour De France when the winner's jersey is presented each day by two of the local women, I've seen better woman working in a Russian quarry. And they all have funny legs, you can spot a French woman a mile off by her legs, even Mooweeelle had funny legs in spite of her hips. But there's something about them. Something a bit sexy, a bit promising…you just know they are capable of doing something a little dirty. The way they walk and particularly the way they sit, I can forgive them anything after five minutes of watching them sit.

Now was the time to evaluate my research into woman's breasts. There had been little point in the orient because they don't hardly have breasts at all and in the Middle East you sure as hell can't see anything of them. But Frenchwomen! The young and indeed the not so young all wear these crop tops and further as they stroll elegantly along the boulevards they keep one hand on their upper stomachs keeping their blouses pressed firmly against their bodies so the material is stretched tightly over their breasts. To a Frenchwoman her breasts are all about sex. They know it and proclaim it proudly, they even pause as they go past you and give a half turn so you can view them from all sides. The watching Frenchmen raise their glasses or coffee cups in acknowledgement but I'm a anally retentive Englishman who has to take brief furtive glances under the disguise of reading a newspaper. Hm, perhaps the French have got something right at last, even if they can't do onion soup. Still, it considerably enlivened my day ashore.

    And then it was back to the ship and back to Carol's thing! Wonderful! Wonderful! Wonderful! And I thought the cruise had gone cold! This was bar none the greatest entertainment I had on the whole cruise taking into account both Sootu and Mooweeelle. A week ago the staff had put on an amateur performance, all of them doing variety acts, you know the sort of thing. Now it was the crew's turn and Carol, the star of the staff's show, had been asked to choreograph the main musical number. To be fair Carol is a very good singer with a powerful voice and she sings songs of great complexity. Sometimes she just picks up the mike in one of the bars and accompanies the pianist with a casuality that leaves me both admiring and jealous. For the crew's thing she had put together this Fred and Ginger number, you know the one: **Flying Down To Rio.** There were a dozen girls and two men with Carol in the centre organising it all. They were having a full rehearsal at one in the morning before presenting it the following day to the passengers and this was the one Carol had asked me to attend. They had been having some trouble with the song because some of the singers couldn't agree on where to stand on the somewhat restricted stage and if you remember the piece they are all supposed to be flapping around on the wings of an aeroplane. Carol had drawn up a plan and she thought she had solved all the problems but she wanted me to sit in the auditorium to ensure that the audience could see all the performers and to study all the mannerisms, stuff like that.

Well, it started off fine, I was very impressed by the professionalism of the whole thing so I was just sitting back and opening up a bag of popcorn when things started to go in a direction Carol hadn't necessarily intended when she choreographed it. They're about half way through the: ***Owow Rio, myow Rio***, bit when it becomes apparent that two of the girls are trying to edge in front of one another. One finally manages to upstage the other by getting herself into a position that completely blocks out the other's face. Suddenly, the faceless one leaves off singing, rushes forward and gives her opponent an enormous shove that sends her skittering across the stage on her enormous heels and she disappears into the wings with an appalling crash. Shit, thought I, that must mean multiple fractures at least if indeed she hasn't killed her! Not a bit of it, the crew are a lot tougher than the staff and she comes barrelling back onto the stage howling like a gorilla and goes for her singing partner like Clinton for a call girl. In seconds they are really at it, shoes and bits of hair are everywhere, and all the other singers are gathered around in a cheering hoard egging them on: 'Go on, use your left girl!' 'You've got her down now stick that boot in!' 'Wow, nice one…get that stitched!' That sort of thing. But the best bit was Carol, a true trooper to the last, plodding gamely on irrespective of the carnage that is going on all around: 'Oh Rio, oh my Rio!' Magnificent! Better than a ***Two Ronnies*** sketch any day.

I was left lying helpless in my chair, the popcorn all spilled away, too weak to move. It was some ten minutes

before I was able to stagger back to my cabin and I lay awake for hours and I bet I woke the guy in the next cabin again. The following morning I went down to see Carol in the library to give her my commiserations but when she grudgingly told me that they had been taken off for: ***artistic differences*** I completely lost it again and ran howling from the library. I tried twice more, wearing my serious face, but each time I saw her I dissolved. The last time I went she threw a signed copy of **Bill Bryson** at me.
    Wonderful! Wonderful! Wonderful!

41 Southampton

And so it comes right down to the last day and it is time to pack. I've said all my goodbyes, difficult ones to Paula and Daniella and to the dozens of crew and staff who have befriended me over the last four months, it's going to be like leaving my family behind. But fortunately it's going to be low key because the cruise doesn't end until New York so I'm going to miss all the last night parties and other stuff. I can just slip away unnoticed.

I visit the left luggage office and ask for my bags and cabin trunk and there is some consternation. There is much whispering in corners and false smiles in my direction and promises to deliver them to my cabin within the hour. Thirty five minutes later a be suited Filipino arrives at my door with a clipboard and a crestfallen expression on his face, apparently my suitcases have disappeared. I ask about the cabin trunk and there he is more sure of his ground: they know for certain that my trunk was put ashore either in Sydney or Hong Kong. The be suited one is highly nervous at imparting this news and I remember my reputation for not suffering fools at all, let alone gladly. I smile at him and thank him sincerely for his help and he rushes off after promising to fix everything for me.

A sense of relief now washes over me because I had been dreading wasting my last day packing and now I didn't have to so I went swimming instead. When I returned Lito was waiting outside my cabin with that shattered look on his face, he told me he had come to escort me to the **Harrods** store on board where I was to choose all the replacement luggage I needed. I thanked him and asked him about the letter he must have had that morning but no, it wasn't the thought of his family that was devastating him it was my missing luggage. Lito had signed for it, Lito had supposedly taken it to the luggage store and now Lito was responsible for it. He had to pay for a new set of luggage at the QE2s impossible prices…it would no doubt wipe out all he had earned on the entire cruise.

    I visited the purser and withdrew my complaint. I told him my cases were only old ones anyway and I had little need of a cabin trunk without a cabin (or indeed a house) to put it in. The purser was very nice about it (he was lying though, he knew there was no way I would have let Lito pay for a new set) and he assured me that a complaint to Cunard would garner compensation (it did as well). He also said he would have some plastic bags delivered to my cabin to put my stuff in and furthermore he shook my hand and told me he'd enjoyed having me aboard.

    We were arriving at Southampton in the evening so I went and shoved everything into the blue plastic bags except for what I was wearing and put them outside the door of my cabin and had a nap.

    It was quite exciting, I hid it well but I was looking forward to seeing my daughter again, and my mother, who had unfailing written a letter to be waiting at every single port of call…something that had moved me to tears for the first half of the cruise until I had dumped the Prozac. We pulled very slowly in and at last Big C announced that we could disembark. I looked around the little cabin I had lived in for the last four months and the tatty little porthole which I had never been able to see anything out of then with a sigh I picked up the four paintings I had purchased aboard and made my way ashore for the last time. I tried to sneak away but waiting at the gangplank was Paula and

Daniella and about another dozen of the crew. Strange, all my friends were from the crew, the only passenger I had made a real friend of was Ardy and she had got off in Egypt. Carol wasn't there, which was hardly surprising because she thought I was on until New York, so after another round of crying I finally stepped ashore.

My luggage wasn't there with all the others. John and June were shepparding a huge stack of cases but they came and thanked me and we swapped addresses and then they were off and the pile of luggage was getting smaller and smaller. I found the baggage officer and told him that mine should be easy to spot because it was all in blue bags and he gave me that false smile again and rushed away. I was left waiting for ages and I started to fume, my daughter would be waiting outside customs for me, she was never late. At last he came back with dragging heels and an assistant purser. What had I packed my baggage in? Where had I left it? What time was this? And then the false smiles again and the purser cleared his throat. The blue bags I had been issued with were rubbish bags as those were the only ones available and I had put them outside my cabin, as instructed, just before the refuse collecting service had come around. I asked carefully what had happened to them and after a moment or two of throat clearing he informed me that it appeared that they had been thrown over the side with all the other rubbish while we had been at sea. He then gave another false smile and edged behind the baggage officer. The baggage officer had the solution though, he gave me a claim form which I had to fill in and submit to Cunard.

I studied the form for a long moment and cleared my throat: 'So, what you are saying is that all my baggage, that is, all the possessions I have left in the world, have been chucked into the Atlantic?' The baggage officer gave me a reassuring smile, 'Well, no' he said, 'strictly speaking it was The Channel.' 'Oh,' said I, 'that's okay then, I thought I was in trouble.' 'But, I'm sure that Cunard will fully compensate you, sir,' said the assistant purser over the other man's shoulder. 'Right,' I said. Then I added, 'Thank you,' because it seemed only polite. I turned and hoisted my four paintings under my arm and staggered off towards customs.

There was a line of seven custom officers waiting for me and I marched past them carrying four paintings on which I was required to pay duty. They eyed me up and down and I did the same to them then I went on walking. I distinctly heard the end one say to his nearest companion: 'He looks a bit obvious don't he?' I dunno, a custom's officer and he can't get his grammar right and I thought I'd got problems.

In the exit building I gazed around and there was a blackboard up with my name on it and a desk number. Apparently I had a message…my daughter had broken down on the orbital and would be two hours late.

I looked around for a seat but there wasn't one so I piled my paintings against the wall and took stock: I'd lost all my possessions, all my clothes except for the one's I was wearing and four paintings, for the Poison Dwarf would have surely disposed of anything I had left behind. I had left my car with my daughter so that would now be a wreck. I had no money left at all, I had spent the very last in giving my Filipino friends tips. And there was no one to meet me.

An enormous warm feeling of freedom came washing over me, I could go anywhere, I could do anything…I could start all over again! How many people get that chance in life? Suddenly I started to laugh!

If you have enjoyed this book by Nicholas Walker the follow up to it where Nick goes to California is called: *Not Quite Sane in America* and his further misadventures are related in: *Losing My Marbles in LA* both available on Kindle.
Then coming in 2017: *Totally Off The Twig In The Middle East* when Nick runs away again and ends up teaching in Iraq.

Not Quite Sane in America

Extracts:

'Finger up your bottom I'm afraid, Dr Walker,' said the man in the white coat.

'I should cocoa!' said I.

'But…well, you have to,' he said half amused, half annoyed.

'You simply 'aint big enough pal,' said I, in my most Clint-like voice.

'Well, I can't force you,' he said snapping the file on me closed with a frustrated click. He turned for a

Parthian shot: 'But, the surgeon will have to do it anyway!'…

…'You checked yourself out?' my daughter demanded, her eyes flashing dangerously.

'No, I was discharged,' I said.

'The hospital has just rung up,' she smashed my argument to pieces with one stroke of her barrister trained tongue.

'Ah,' said I. Not my best retort but I'd had a trying day.

'And they want their drip back,' she added.

'It's in the cafe toilets,' I admitted.

'You don't even know how to remove a drip…you must be potty!'

'I watch ER a lot.'

She came up and took me by the arm and put on that patient look she has been using with me since she was about four.

'Listen Dad, it was a perfectly routine operation that millions of people have every year, you don't have to be embarrassed about it.'

'Absolutely,' I said my responses gathering maturity.

'Now, I've got to go and fetch Jessica from school then we are going to run you back to hospital. They've got a bed for you waiting.'

'Is it asking for me personally?'

'Probably. You're going to be there for at least a week,' her voice dropped to dramatize her next words: 'and even then you have to go in daily for examination for at least another month.'

'You mean they want to look up my bottom every single day for a month?' I demanded aghast.

'Of course they do,' she said. Then added quite unnecessarily, 'Doesn't everybody?' She squeezed my arm which meant she was either trying to reassure me or "borrow" money again, 'Listen Dad, it's time to be sensible, this is serious you know. This is your health you are talking about here, you can't run away from this. You collapsed in Petra and again in Penzance, they had to send an ambulance.'

I hung my head, 'I know,' I said. 'Don't worry, I'm not entirely stupid you know.'

'No,' she said a bit too hurriedly. She glanced at her watch, 'Look, I've really got to go, Jessica will kill me if I'm late again…I'll be back in about half an hour.'

I carefully walked her to the car and she flashed me a last anxious smile and I gave her a reassuring wave…then I grabbed up my hospital rucksack, swiped a cushion from her couch and ran away to America…

…There came a frantic scurrying on the stairs and a frenzied hammering on my door. I opened it to find a little man dancing up and down: 'Ooo, you've filled up my gallery with smelly water!' he sort of howls at me. Well, I tried to be sympathetic but it was the smelly water part that really got to me and I collapsed hooting on the bed (still the towels). 'It's all very well,' he shouts, 'but I'm having a party tonight!' I couldn't think of any action I could take that would improve the situation so I offered him some pizza. 'I don't eat Pizza! I don't eat cheese or anything like that. I'm a vegan.' Well stap me, there's a surprise! It was a big pizza with lots of bacon and onions and extra tomatoes and cheese and stuff and I wasn't even half way through it when a man in blue overalls arrived carrying the biggest screwdriver you have ever seen in your life. I thought he was a hit-man sent by Peter to screw me to death. He asks to look at the bathroom and he wanders around a bit. I offer him some pizza but he apparently doesn't eat when he's working (you can see his point of view what with where he has to stick his hands). He asks me what had happened and I told him about the *Draino* and he nods understandingly then he asks if I am British and when I say yes he seems to think this explains everything. He says my plumbing seems to be ok but I've blown apart a conduit in Peter's gallery. Next to arrive is a fireman, sorry firefighter. He isn't a great conversationist more of a grunter, he has a quick look in my bathroom, advises me to leave the window open for the rest of the day and refuses a piece of pizza. He then asks me if I am British and grunts understandingly when I admit this.

    I finally finish my pizza and decide to go and have a sleep on the beach, I might get some peace there what with plumbers and firefighters keeping on banging on my door. When I get downstairs the firefighter is taping up the door to Peter's gallery with yellow tape with: *Official, Fire Department. Do Not Cross* printed on it. Peter is jumping up and down protesting about the party he's holding later that evening: 'Well, you won't be holding it in there,' said my friend the grunting firefighter. I sneaked past feeling my presence wasn't needed at that precise moment.

    Well, the party had to go on so he held it in the little courtyard below, it's quite a nice little courtyard all lit by fairy (ha, I wonder if Peter puts them up) lights, but it was hardly the place to hold a champagne art viewing. I carried my deckchair out onto my stairway to watch (I couldn't take the padded chair in case The Spaniard was there). Oh, it was wonderful! All these women in cocktail dresses and all these blokes in floppy suits drinking Champagne and trying to pretend they weren't all crammed in a sad little courtyard. But the best bit was that when it came to your turn to view Peter's latest works you had to go and stand on this wobbly upturned flower pot and peer through a dirty little window: 'I'm very pleased with my *Rising Sunset,* you can see most of it just behind the pillar.' The sight of those women in their tight little dresses and high heels clambouring up onto that pot will keep me happy for months. There is only one thing that worries me, why didn't anyone want a piece of my pizza? Do they know something about *Domino's Pizzas* that I don't?...

    ...The apartment was on the third floor. I briefly glanced at the elevator but three Hispanic youths were using it as a kinda coffee bar and were smoking some flowery smelling cigarettes. I felt disinclined to disturb them so I plodded up the stairs and soon found myself standing outside a metal door that looked like it belonged on a safe. It was all dented and paint was sprayed on it. There didn't seem to be a doorbell so I knocked on it as politely as I could.

After a disappointing wait I was forced to knock again and this time used my fist, even that didn't seem to make much of an impression on this reinforced portal but all of a sudden it shot open. I blinked, a short, but very wide Hispanic woman was standing there. She wasn't unattractive if you like your female company shaped more like a bulldozer than a Mini Cooper, her shoulders seemed to stretch from one side of the doorway to the other and her upper arms were particularly impressive!

'Who're you?' she demanded looking me up and down as though I smelt nasty.

'Hi, my name is Nicholas Walker,' I supplied.

'Wha you want?'

'I believe a young man named Gabriel lives here.'

'You cops?'

'No. It's Doctor Nicholas Walker,' I said with a reassuring smile. 'May I speak to him, please?'

'Wha about?' she demanded, 'Me mother.'

'Ah, I'm pleased to meet you,' I said but I wasn't about to get a handshake. 'I understand that your son may have some idea where my bike is. It disappeared from outside The Holiday Inn in Burbank.'

She turned and emitted a below like Town Crier: 'Gabby, get ass out here!' Well, I'd have obeyed that instruction with as much alacrity as possible and her son was no exception. A scrawny youth of about sixteen appeared looking scared. She grabbed him by the hair and pulled his face right up to hers.

'You steal bikes again?' she howled. 'I tell you 'bout running with them boys.' She was making the most incredible amount of noise so the denials and the pleas of her son went completely unheard. 'You li' bastard!' she shrieked and obviously considering that corporal punishment was an option to be pursued in this case she brought her fist around in a massive blow that crumpled the poor sod up like a dandelion clock in a thunderstorm. She changed to Spanish and found she could express herself even more volubly and, although I wouldn't have thought it possible, her voice reached a new level. She reached down and dragged him upright by the hair and now she started to slap him around like he was an ill-behaved cart horse. It sounded just like when your tyre gets ripped off when you are doing about eighty: ***Flump! Flump! Flump! Flump!***

'Madam, please,' I interjected, for as prejudiced as I was against this young man this was getting too much. She turned to look at me as though she had never seen me before in her life: 'You fuck off!' she said then she slammed the door in my face like an executioner locking the gas chamber for the final time. The howling and slapping sounds started up again from behind the thick metal. Oh well!

'What we had there,' I said, 'was a failure to communicate.'

Printed in Great Britain
by Amazon